FRONTIER ADAPTATIONS
IN LOWER CENTRAL AMERICA

FRANKLIN O. LOVELAND teaches anthropology at Gettysburg College. He received his M.A. and Ph.D. from Duke University after field work among the Shouters of Trinidad and the Rama Indians of Nicaragua, and has written a number of papers about the cultural symbolism and mythology of these groups. His most recent field work was at an Indian school in Minnesota.

Frontier Adaptations

in Lower Central America

Mary W. Helms / Franklin O. Loveland
editors

A Publication of the
Institute for the Study of Human Issues
Philadelphia

Manufactured in the United States of America

Library of Congress Cataloging in Publication Data:

Main entry under title:

Frontier adaptations in lower Central America.

Essays originally presented at the 9th annual meeting of the Southern
Anthropological Society in April 1974.
Bibliography: p.
Includes index.
1. Indians of Central America—Congresses. 2. Central America—Social
conditions—Congresses. I. Helms, Mary W. II. Loveland, Franklin O. III.
Southern Anthropological Society.
F1434.F76   301.29′728   76–25073
ISBN 0–915980–55–X

For information, write:

Director of Publications
ISHI
3401 Science Center
Philadelphia, Pennsylvania 19104
U.S.A.

Contents

Part Three
NATIVE ADAPTATIONS TO AN ECONOMIC HINTERLAND

FRONTIER ADAPTATIONS
IN LOWER CENTRAL AMERICA

Introduction

MARY W. HELMS

The anthropological study of Middle America has progressed through several stages during the last three decades. The papers published in 1940 in *The Maya and Their Neighbors* (Hay et al. 1940) evidence a general concern with indigenous culture traits from northern Mexico to Colombia. But twelve years later the Viking Fund Seminar on Middle American Ethnology focused mainly on native culture patterns of central-southern Mexico and Guatemala, the region defined by Kirchhoff as "Mesoamerica" (Kirchhoff 1952; Tax et al. 1952: 283). This emphasis continued into the 1960s. Indeed, during these years "Middle America" was virtually equated with "Mesoamerica" (cf. Willey and Phillips 1958: 20, 147n; Wolf 1959). Even the *Handbook of Middle American Indians* (Wauchope 1964–), which formally includes northern Mexico and lower Central America, has focused primarily on Mesoamerica, undoubtedly because anthropological knowledge of the societies of northern Mexico and especially lower Central America is markedly more limited than information about the Mesoamerican heartland. Within the last ten to fifteen years, however, a growing number of ethnographic, ethnohistorical, and archaeological investigations have been conducted into these Mesoamerican "frontiers." As a result, the anthropological horizons of "Middle America" are slowly being extended again to include material not only from northern Mexico (whose relevance for Mesoamerican studies has been recognized for quite some time) but also from lower Central America.[1]

The essays in this volume, which were originally presented at the Ninth Annual Meeting of the Southern Anthropological Society in April 1974, reflect this growing interest in Central America south of Guatemala and El Salvador. The subjects are varied, a result of the diverse orientations of contemporary anthropology and of the many

1

unexplored areas of investigation in lower Central American studies. In spite of this seeming eclecticism, however, common themes can be identified. I should like briefly to consider the most significant and all-pervasive of these themes, that of lower Central America as a cultural hinterland or frontier of areas immediately to the north and south and of more distant North American and European nations.

In its broadest sense the study of frontiers is concerned with the great diversity of situations and relationships which result when culturally distinct groups of people meet. From these meetings complex intergroup interactions involving the ebb and flow of trade and exchange, raids and warfare, and political alliance may result. Each of these various types of frontier interaction contains distinctive characteristics. However, the identification of specific frontier interactions and analysis of their frequently complicated interplay have hardly begun in lower Central American studies. Therefore, in presenting an outline of Central American culture history, I shall use a broad approach based on the trilogy of meanings that have been given to the term "frontier," as noted by Wyman and Kroeber:

> Man has been a wanderer, and . . . has moved restlessly into new lands and against the border of other men's domains. The farthest limits of his advance have been called the frontier, a term describing so many situations that its meaning has become vague. . . . Considering the great variety of frontiers, it is small wonder that historians have no fixed meaning of the term. They have considered it *a place, or a process, or a situation.* A frontier may mean a primitive people that live beyond a settled society, the movement of an aggressive people into the lands of a simpler folk called barbarians, military or trading posts in the borderland, or even the time and place where institutions are adapted to new conditions [1957: xiii; my italics].

Keeping in mind the concept of frontiers of place, of process, and of situation, let us briefly discuss the culture history of lower Central America in the pre-Columbian, colonial, and republican eras.

The Pre-Columbian Era

The term "lower Central America" refers to an area comprising eastern Honduras, eastern Nicaragua, Costa Rica, and Panama. At times Belize or British Honduras is included. The geographical arena where frontier contacts occurred can be conveniently divided, as shown in Figure 1, into three major physiographical provinces: the

Caribbean lowlands, generally warm and humid tropical forest or savannah; the somewhat drier Pacific coastal plains and volcanic uplands; and the central highlands, which form a mountainous backbone along the length of Central America (cf. West and Augelli 1966: Chapter 2). During the pre-Columbian era these highlands and lowlands witnessed the evolution of a number of small tribes and chiefdoms. The course of development is still poorly understood, for archaeological investigations remain in their infancy for much of the region. Nonetheless, by A.D. 500 small rank societies are evident in Panama and Costa Rica, while the peoples of the Caribbean lowlands of eastern Nicaragua and Honduras apparently never passed the egalitarian (tribal) level of sociopolitical integration (cf. Baudez 1963).

By virtue of linguistic ties with the Chibchan language family and a number of specific culture traits of South American affinity, the indigenous cultures of lower Central America have generally been considered part of the Intermediate Area, a culture area including lower Central America and northern South America and so named because of its geographical location between the two high-culture areas of Mesoamerica and the Central Andes (Rouse 1962; Willey 1971: 256–258). Furthermore, in general discussions of pre-Columbian culture history the societies of this so-called Intermediate Area are frequently considered as lying "beyond" the productive heartlands of pre-Columbian civilization (Sanders and Price 1968: 57, 172–173; Meggers 1972: 45, 100; Rouse 1962: 56; Willey 1966: 144–145).

A closer look, however, reveals that the societies of lower Central America were, in fact, significantly involved with neighboring "heartland" areas, particularly Mesoamerica (Strong 1940; Myers 1973; Willey 1971: 348–352). Though apparently situated beyond reach of political controls by Mesoamerican states and "empires," lower Central America probably had a stronger economic association with Mesoamerican regions than the sparse and fragmentary archaeological and ethnohistoric data suggest. Ceramics and goldwork indicate contact and exchange with the Mayan lowlands of the Petén and Yucatán (Lothrop 1952; Coe 1962; Pendergast 1970; Stone 1972: 150–151). Ties with Mesoamerican highlands can be seen in ceramics, stonework, and metallurgy (Lothrop 1966: 197, 207; Stone 1972: 167–174 *passim*). Sites along the *linea vieja,* the old railroad line of north-central Costa Rica, have revealed what appears to be a center of exchange between Mesoamerica and lower Central America, perhaps one that operated along the manner of "ports of trade" (Chapman

Figure 1   Political and Physiographical Regions of Central America

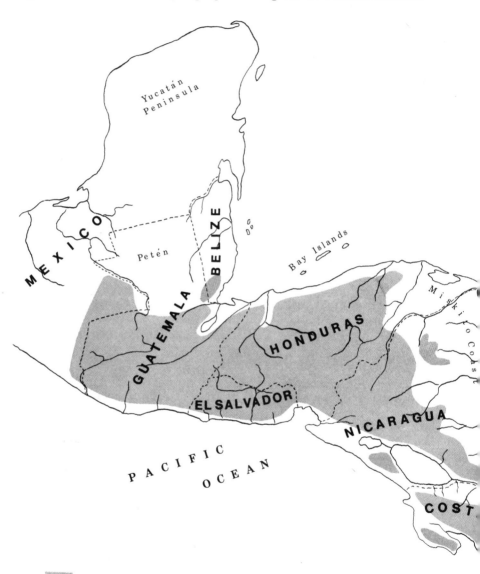

Yucatán
Peninsula

MEXICO

Petén

BELIZE

GUATEMALA

Bay Islands

HONDURAS

Miskito Coast

EL SALVADOR

NICARAGUA

PACIFIC

OCEAN

COST

MOUNTAINS AND HIGHLANDS

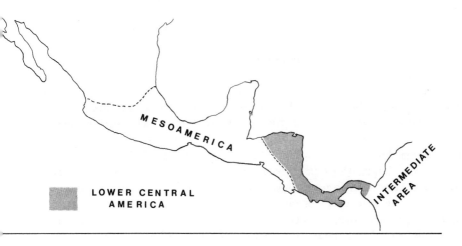

MESOAMERICA

LOWER CENTRAL
AMERICA

INTERMEDIATE
AREA

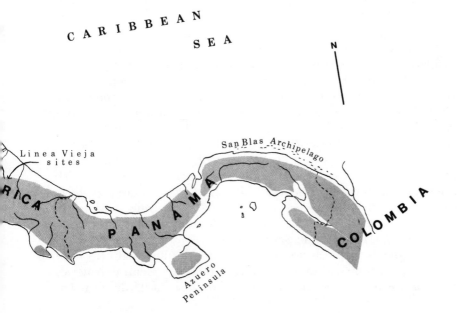

CARIBBEAN
SEA

N

Linea Vieja
sites

San Blas Archipelago

RICA

PANAMA

COLOMBIA

Azuero
Peninsula

1957). Here a great diversity of shell, stone, ceramic, and metallurgi-
cal items has been found with affinities to northern South America,
the West Indies, Mesoamerica, and even Peru (Lothrop 1955; Stone
1972: 26–29, 95–99, 155; Stone and Balser 1965). Trade routes by sea
between Yucatán and the Isthmus of Panama are also indicated
(Lothrop 1940: 428).

Hispanic documents further indicate that colonies of "foreigners," quite likely Mesoamericans, were established at various points in
lower Central America, including: the region of Nombre de Dios in
Panama; the Pacific coast of Panama west of the Azuero Peninsula; an
area near the mouth of the Sigua (Sixaola) River of southeastern
Costa Rica; the mouth of the Río San Juan in southeastern Nicaragua;
and eastern Honduras (Lothrop 1926: 9, 1942; Sauer 1966: 270–272,
275; Stone 1972: 194–198 *passim;* see also Minelli's chapter in this
volume). The intentions of these groups are unknown, but it is likely
that economic interests were involved. It also has been suggested that
had the Spanish Conquest been delayed lower Central America might
have fallen under a measure of Mesoamerican political control, particularly by the Mexica (Aztec) empire (Lothrop 1942: 114–115; Stone
1972: 208). While it may be questioned whether the Mexica would
have been capable of effecting and maintaining such far-flung political expansion, it is clear that significant ties existed between the tribes
and chiefdoms of Central America and their powerful Mesoamerican
neighbors.[2]

Relatively little is known of the relationships between lower Central American societies and peoples of northern South America, although an active interchange probably existed for many centuries,
particularly with Colombia, the "heartland" of the Intermediate Area
(Kidder 1940). Archaeological data reveal ceramic ties, commonalities
in burial practices, and a considerable exchange of high-status prestige items, including precious stones and goldpieces, between Colombia and Panama-Costa Rica (Kidder 1940; Myers 1973; Reichel-
Dolmatoff 1965: 120–121, 132; Stone 1972: 174, 186). These data
raise questions regarding travel routes and modes of exchange which
have barely been touched (Myers 1973). Ethnohistoric sources, however, indicate that a network of riverways, land trails, and ocean
routes connected the isthmus with Colombia, primarily via the Río
Atrato system (Helms n.d.b; Sauer 1966).

It should be possible to ascertain some institutional effects of
frontier contact on cultures reaching into lower Central America
from outside and on societies indigenous to the area. Little study has

been made of this question, but a few general comments can be made. State institutional forms characteristic of Mesoamerica were unable to survive as such in lower Central America, where levels of local sociopolitical integration did not evolve beyond that of chiefdom or tribe. Lothrop (1940: 427) and Palerm and Wolf (1960: 6–9) have noted that Mesoamerican traditions tended to become simpler and to acculturate to local patterns on the southern peripheries of Mesoamerica and in lower Central America (Stone 1972). Similarly, more distant Mesoamerican colonies at Sigua, near the Sixaola River, and Nombre de Dios, on the Caribbean coast of Panama, failed to become permanently established (Lothrop 1942; Sauer 1966: 239).

On the other hand, work in progress indicates that contacts between lower Central America and Mesoamerica or northern South America may have stimulated a higher level of chiefdom development among some Panamanian rank societies than otherwise would have occurred. Ethnohistoric evidence suggests that those Panamanian chiefs whose domains were situated at major junctions of the travel routes connecting Panama with Mesoamerica and Colombia achieved a greater degree and range of power, influence, and wealth than did their more isolated colleagues (Helms n.d.b).

The Colonial Era

With the discovery of the New World and the subsequent exploration, conquest, and settlement by Spanish conquistadors and colonists, the frontier status of lower Central America assumed new complexities. The Central American societies now faced new contact agencies: Spanish conquerors and missionaries as well as British traders and settlers, Spain's rivals for the wealth of the Indies.

The Spanish arrived first, and for a decade (1510–1520) Panama stood in the forefront of exploration and conquest (Sauer 1966). The riches of Mexico and Peru, however, soon drew the avaricious Iberians away from the limited material wealth of the isthmus, leaving it a devastated hinterland of limited Hispanic colonization. Spanish settlements elsewhere in lower Central America (in Costa Rica, Nicaragua, and Honduras) differed from those in Panama and from each other mainly in their degree of poverty and provincialism, for these colonies represented the southern hinterland of the viceroyalty of New Spain, which was centered in Mexico City and in the Mesoamerican heartland. Although the colonies were officially linked administratively to the viceroy and the Spanish crown, distance and difficult communications limited effective contact with central authorities, and the Spanish colonists of lower Central America were forced to regulate their own affairs more or less by themselves. This condition engendered much dissension and conflict among and within the respective colonies, and the organizational problems, together with limited native resources and limited mineral wealth, did not recommend the hinterland provinces to newcomers from Spain (MacLeod 1973; Chamberlain 1966; Bancroft 1886).

These difficulties also restricted the geographical extent of effective Spanish settlement and control in Central America. Permanent Spanish settlements were located virtually without exception in the more temperate Pacific plains and uplands of Central America. Although Spain claimed formal authority over all Central American territory, in fact the central mountains and the Caribbean lowlands from eastern Yucatán to Colombia remained unconquered and unsettled by Hispanic peoples. Initial Spanish explorations had found these regions lacking in mineral wealth, unsuitable for Spanish forms of agriculture, and populated by hostile natives who, in the absence of greater incentives, were not worth subduing (cf. Floyd 1967; Bancroft 1886).

Though Spaniards failed to colonize these distant reaches, other Europeans, mainly British, succeeded in doing so. Small settlements of English planters, logwood cutters, and traders emerged along the Caribbean coast from Yucatán to Colombia, while the many hidden coves and streams sheltered more fleeting communities of privateers and buccaneers. Eventually England claimed portions of this territory (eastern Nicaragua and eastern Honduras—the so-called Miskito Coast—and Belize in eastern Yucatán) as a protectorate (cf. Floyd 1967; MacLeod 1973; Bancroft 1886).

The colonial landscape of lower Central America thus was resolved into two, or more accurately three, frontier territories: a western or Pacific sector controlled by Spanish colonists; an eastern or Caribbean coastal sector thinly settled by English-speaking peoples and indigenous natives; and a strip of interior mountainous country, between the Spaniards and the British, still populated only by indigenous peoples. From their respective bases Spaniards, English, and Indians evolved various networks of contact, cooperation, and conflict.

For the crown of Spain and the crown of England the basic issue regarding Central America concerned the legality of English efforts to become involved in economic activities in these regions, for Spain asserted legal monopoly over all commercial matters involving territories she claimed, while England denied such monopolies if they could not be enforced (Solnick 1970: Chapters 4 and 6; Stein and Stein 1970: Part I). At the local level the issue was defined in more immediate terms. The Spanish colonists of western Central America stood in need of many manufactured goods that they could obtain only in limited quantity and at great cost through the official Spanish mercantile channels centered in distant Mexico City and Seville. English traders settled across the mountains on the Caribbean shore were anxious to provide these goods in exchange for local resources from Spanish Central America. Consequently a thriving contraband trade arose between English and Spanish settlers, and lasted for the duration of the colonial era (MacLeod 1973: Chapter 20; Woodward 1965: 553–556).

Periodically, however, this relatively peaceful frontier exchange was interrupted by more militant interactions. During the first half of the seventeenth century English privateers raided Spanish settlements in Central America and the Caribbean. In the second half of the century free-lance buccaneers of diverse origins operating from secluded settlements on the isolated Central American Caribbean shore and from Jamaica and Tortuga attacked Spanish outposts and such leading colonial towns as Panama City, León, and Granada (Bancroft 1886; Haring 1910; Solnick 1970: 65–74).

The pirates' success in Central America owed much to the cooperation of native peoples, particularly the Cuna of eastern Panama and the Miskito of eastern Nicaragua and Honduras. These Indians served as guides and provisioners for pirate parties, sometimes traveling great distances with the raiders for months or even years at a time (Helms 1971: 15; Stout 1947: 51). In return for their invaluable services Miskito and Cuna received loot from the attacks and various European trade goods including guns and ammunition. With these new armaments the Miskito became a scourge in their own right, launching raids into the interior of Honduras, Nicaragua, and Costa Rica against other native peoples, and attacking Spanish settlements to obtain captives and loot which they then exchanged with British traders for more European ammunition, cloth, iron tools, foodstuffs, and so on (Helms 1969).

A few additional points should be noted concerning the Miskito. These so-called Indians are a biologically mixed people originating during the colonial period from miscegenation between indigenous women of eastern Nicaragua and British settlers, buccaneers, and especially Negro freemen and slaves who sought the isolated shore as refugees from Spanish and West Indian colonies or were brought to the coast as laborers by English planters. In cultural terms, however, the Miskito maintained their native language and followed indigenous customs to a great extent (Helms 1971: 17–19; Helms in press; see also Davidson's chapter in this volume).

Faced with smuggling, pirate raids, and Indian attacks, Central American Spanish officials planned a formidable defense calling for construction of forts at various points (generally on waterways) along the Spanish frontier. The plan also included the establishment of a chain of missions near the interior mountains to resettle the natives of these regions in Hispanic mission communities, so as to form a buffer zone against the more distant Miskito. Neither approach was successful. The forts failed to halt smuggling or to repulse pirates, while the missions were attacked by Miskito raiders and their religious neophytes fled to mountain refuges (Floyd 1967).

Although the general nature of colonial-era interactions among Indians, Spaniards, and English can be traced, it has proved more difficult to identify the various adjustments that these diverse frontier activities forced upon the customs and institutions of the indigenous inhabitants and upon the various European colonial groups entering the region. The institutional adjustments are of particular importance, since to a considerable degree the institutional forms seen today among native peoples of the central mountains and Caribbean lowlands (as well as aspects of the Hispanic culture patterns characteristic of the Pacific regions) are based on adaptations emanating from colonial frontier situations. Although much work remains to be done on this subject, broad areas of adaptation can be noted.

The colonial provinces of Hispanic Central America reveal fascinatingly diverse responses to common problems. Modes of provincial administration, the composition of colonial society, and the relative availability and degree of distribution of wealth all varied among the respective Hispanic colonies. To a greater or lesser extent these factors reflected the type of indigenous society encountered by the Spaniards in western Central America and the reactions of the native peoples to Spanish conquest.

In western Guatemala Hispanic control of the densely populated native states was essentially achieved by replacing native rulers with Spanish administrators without destroying the family and community orientations of native society. Thus colonial Guatemalan society came to be divided between a numerically small but powerful Hispanic elite and a very large lower sector of natives whose labor supported the elite in wealth and comfort (MacLeod 1973).

Under the force of European conquest the native chiefdoms of western Nicaragua, western Honduras, and El Salvador, inherently more fragile organizationally, were unable to maintain indigenous institutions as successfully as the native states in Guatemala. In addition European diseases, forced labor in mines, and large-scale shipment as slaves to Panama and Peru seriously depleted the native population (MacLeod 1973). Consequently, there were fewer Indians available to support the Spanish elite and control of these laborers yielded less wealth to the colonial upper sector. Miscegenation between Spaniards and Indians was more frequent, too, and the native segment of society gradually was replaced by a growing number of mestizos (Stanger 1932; Karnes 1961: Chapter 1).

In western Costa Rica warfare and European diseases had broken the native chiefdoms and reduced the indigenous population even before permanent European colonization was achieved. As the Spanish threat advanced, surviving natives fled to the safety of the mountains, particularly the Talamancan range, where their descendants, known today collectively as the Talamanca Indians, still remain (Stone 1962), as Figure 2 indicates. Little Indian labor and few Indian women remained for Spanish exploitation. Therefore Costa Rica became a colony of relatively poor, self-sufficient Spanish small farmers who tilled the soil themselves to meet their subsistence needs (MacLeod 1973; Munro 1967: Chapter 7; Stanger 1932). The fate of many Panamanian natives was comparable to that of the western Costa Rican peoples. The Pacific coast chiefdoms of western Panama, where Spanish settlements were located, were particularly hard hit. Those natives who escaped withdrew into the fastnesses of the central cordillera. The Guaymí Indians still resident in the mountains are probably descendants of these refugees (Young 1971: Chapter 2; see also Young's chapter in this volume).

In areas of lower Central America which were not conquered by the Spanish, European contact was less intense and native tribes and chiefdoms achieved more successful adaptations. The chiefdoms of eastern Panama, for example, were less disrupted and had time to effect a more positive adjustment to the new colonial order. To be sure, during the colonial centuries these peoples, now known collectively as Cuna, gradually reduced their territorial hold in order to avoid Spanish contacts, withdrawing across the central mountains

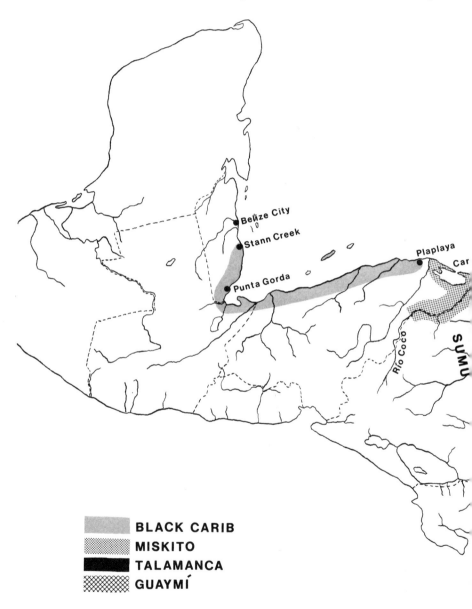

Figure 2 Distribution of Native Peoples of Lower Central America, 1970

BLACK CARIB
MISKITO
TALAMANCA
GUAYMÍ

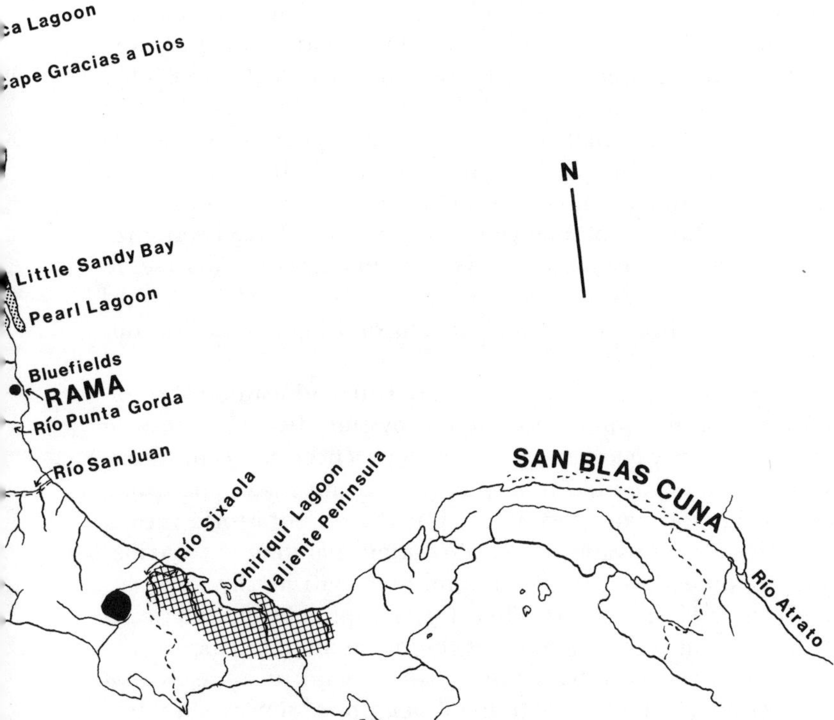

ca Lagoon

Cape Gracias a Dios

N

Little Sandy Bay

Pearl Lagoon

Bluefields

RAMA

Río Punta Gorda

Río San Juan

Río Sixaola

Chiriquí Lagoon

Valiente Peninsula

SAN BLAS CUNA

Río Atrato

until their villages were concentrated on the Caribbean side of eastern Panama (Nordenskiöld 1938; Stout 1947). Yet traditional customs and institutions seem to have been maintained to a considerable extent, at least at the village and family level. Perhaps the greatest change was the gradual diminution of the elite sector of society; these formerly rank societies gradually became more egalitarian. It is possible that one factor leading to the decline of the heredity elite was the breakdown under conquest pressures of the pre-Columbian long-distance exchange networks which had tied the isthmian elite with counterparts in Mesoamerica and northern South America and which had been important means of obtaining high-status items vital to maintaining chiefly positions.[3]

It is also very likely that Cuna residence patterns changed during the colonial centuries, again in response to frontier conditions. Although pre-Columbian data is limited, prior to the Conquest virilocal residence may have been practiced at least by the upper sector of society. However, neolocal ("independent") residence was recorded in the late seventeenth century, while twentieth-century investigators have found uxorilocal residence to be the norm (Stout 1947: 81–82; see Holloman's essay in this volume). In borderlands of the Spanish Empire in the Americas matrilocal residence appears directly correlated with situations in which men were absent from home for lengthy periods of time (Helms 1970). Changes in residence patterns among the Cuna during colonial centuries may well have been a response to opportunities for men to travel with buccaneers and to serve as sailors "voyaging to every principal port in the world... [with] absences of two to three to as much as ten or fifteen years" (Stout 1947: 57).[4]

There are interesting parallels between Cuna adjustments to colonial frontier conditions and those made by the Miskito of eastern Honduras and eastern Nicaragua, who also practiced matrilocal residence by the mid-nineteenth century. Data concerning residence practices prior to this date are very poor, but the ethnohistoric record suggests patrilocal or possibly neolocal residence among these tribes at the time of contact and in no way indicates matrilocality (or matrilineality) (Helms 1971: 25–26). Therefore it cannot be automatically assumed that uxorilocal residence was the norm among tribes of the Miskito coast in pre-Columbian times. Once again, it appears that uxorilocal residence correlates with men's lengthy absences as raiders or as laborers for foreigners at Belize and elsewhere (Helms 1970: 202). (The biological make-up of the Miskito is also significant here, for native women cohabiting with foreign men might be expected to reside either uxorilocally or neolocally, but not virilocally.)

Frontier adaptations also produced territorial changes among the Miskito. However, instead of reducing its territorial extent as did the Cuna, the Miskito population expanded its control of land. The population first identified as Miskito appeared in the vicinity of Cape Gracias a Dios after the mid-seventeenth century. From here Miskito peoples moved into eastern Honduras, south along the Nicaraguan coast, and inland along the Río Coco (Helms 1971: 16–19, 21). This expansion resulted from the acquisition of guns and ammunition and the establishment of English trading posts along the seacoast. With the new weapon the Miskito effectively subdued other indigenous coastal peoples, pushing the survivors, known today collectively as the Sumu, toward the mountainous interior, or, in the case of the Rama, onto islands in Bluefields lagoon (Helms 1971: 20–21; see Loveland's first chapter in this volume). The Miskito then established themselves as middlemen between the interior natives and the English-speaking traders on the coast, exchanging produce obtained from the Sumu, loot from raided Spanish settlements, and products of their own hunting, fishing, and collecting for foreign foods and manufactured goods at the trading posts (Helms 1969). Therefore, in addition to changes in social organization and territorial extent, frontier adaptations during the colonial era in eastern Nicaragua and Honduras also produced significant changes in intersocietal relations among the various indigenous peoples of the region.

The Republican Era

The so-called republican era of Central American culture history began in the early nineteenth century when the Hispanic provinces became politically independent of Spain. However, the new "republics" continued to operate as colonial hinterlands, for Great Britain, Germany, and the United States gradually assumed a high degree of control over Central America's commercial, financial, and political affairs.

Great Britain and the United States were particularly interested in a proposed trans-isthmian canal to be constructed along the Río San Juan and Lake Nicaragua in southern Nicaragua. To emphasize her claim to Central American territory, Great Britain reclaimed eastern Nicaragua and Honduras (the Miskito Coast) as a protectorate.

Although this arrangement was eventually terminated and the Miskito coast formally ceded to Nicaragua and Honduras, Britain maintained a Central American foothold by recognizing the settlement of Belize (British Honduras) as an official colony (Munro 1967: 95–98; Naylor 1960). For its part, the United States asserted its right to become involved in Central American affairs for the sake of its national security. The role of Central America in United States security interests was immensely increased in the early years of the twentieth century when the United States constructed the Panama Canal.

During the late nineteenth century British, United States, and German investors also developed two lucrative cash crops, coffee and bananas, in Central America. Coffee was grown on the Pacific slopes of Central America under the management of the Hispanic elite and with the labor of the rural lower sector. However, marketing operations and financial control were mainly in the hands of British and German bankers and businessmen (Munro 1967: 17–23, 265–268). In the early decades of the twentieth century United States companies, most notably the United Fruit Company and its major competitor, the Standard Fruit and Steamship Company, began to develop banana production in the isolated Central American Caribbean lowlands. Thousands of acres of land were planted, company towns were built, transportation and communication developed (Kepner 1936; Kepner and Soothill 1935; Wilson 1947).

Central American citizens played virtually no role in the production of bananas. North American corporation executives supervised company field managers who, in turn, directed actual operations. Even laborers were imported from outside Central America. The banana companies hired thousands of West Indian Negroes to work on railroads and plantations, and this heavy influx of West Indians added another major non-Hispanic component to the population of the Caribbean lowlands. Even after banana production collapsed in the 1930s and the companies withdrew, many West Indian Negroes remained, living mainly in the small port towns. These "Creoles," as they are termed today, continue to imbue the Caribbean lowlands with a distinctive "Anglo" flavor, for they speak a dialect of English and are predominantly Protestant in religious affiliation (see Cosminsky's essay in this volume on a related English-speaking Black population component of Belize). Since the Creoles maintain strong ties with the British West Indies, the Central American lowlands remain heavily oriented toward the Anglo-Caribbean world, as they were during the seventeenth and eighteenth centuries when they formed part of England's Caribbean sphere of interest (Augelli 1962).

To be sure, residents of the Caribbean lowlands are now citizens of the respective Central American republics (though Belize remains a separate political entity) and technically are subject to the judicial and legislative dictates of these states. The formal contact between lowlands and national centers will probably increase in coming decades, but the Caribbean lowlands likely will remain a hinterland region. Like all of Latin America today, the Central American republics are experiencing runaway population growth. This population explosion is felt most strongly in the Hispanic Pacific sectors which have always been more densely populated than the Caribbean lands. Some of the increase is being absorbed by the capital cities, but population movements have begun to spill across the central mountains and to move down the waterways to the Caribbean lowlands. With these newcomers, of course, come growing pressures to "Hispanicize" the lowlands.

In spite of gradual Hispanicization of the Caribbean areas, the national life of the Central American republics will probably continue to focus on the Pacific Hispanic sector. This is particularly true for matters of national development, such as the mechanized and diversified farming and industrial production that the Central American governments wish to stimulate. Since population (that is, labor), wealth, and resources are more immediately available in the west, effective development efforts are most likely to center here. The Caribbean lowlands, in turn, are likely to continue to evidence subsistence agriculture with traditional techniques and, as the western towns and cities become increasingly modernized, to fall even further behind the Hispanic sectors of the republics (Adams 1967: 99–102).

The events of the nineteenth and twentieth centuries have tended to support the institutional adaptations made by the native peoples of the lowlands during the seventeenth and eighteenth centuries. Both the Cuna and the Miskito, for example, continue to exhibit significant degrees of uxorilocal residence (or village endogamy, which produces the same effect for women), and both retain strong associations with the outside market economy (see the chapters by Cattle, Holloman, and Howe in this volume). Both groups have continued their territorial adjustments as well. The Miskito have become the dominant rural population of eastern Honduras and Nicaragua (Helms 1971: 35), while the Cuna have continued their northward move toward the Caribbean by establishing villages on previously uninhabited islands of the San Blas archipelago, where the majority of the population now reside (Stout 1947: 13).

Yet changes are apparent, too, many of them associated with the

growing importance of wage labor in native life. While economic ex-
changes with European agents in the seventeenth and eighteenth centuries were frequently conducted by barter, nineteenth- and
twentieth-century economic activities have primarily involved cash.
Cash resources, in turn, have encouraged and facilitated the economic independence of wage-earning men and have reduced the
necessity for cooperation and mutual dependence in connection with
the material things of life. Young men able to earn money by their
own efforts are no longer as tightly bound to the extended family, and
may evidence their greater independence by residing virilocally or
neolocally if given the opportunity. Indeed, since many aspects of
interpersonal relations now acquire monetary measure, the solidarity
of the kin group and of social relations in general may be extolled as
an ideal more than actually practiced (Helms 1971: 109).

Nonetheless, counterbalancing factors continue to operate. Duties
of home and family still fall heavily on the women of Cuna and Miskito villages who, through the continued practice of uxorilocal residence, are usually related as mothers, sisters, and daughters. This
core of consanguineally related women is largely responsible for
maintaining the household, particularly when men are laboring at
distant jobs, and for inculcating the traditional language, kin terms,
and forms of kinship respect among the children, who generally continue to speak the mother tongue as their primary language and to
show at least superficially the traditional patterns of kinship obligation and respect as adults (Helms 1970; n.d.a).

It is interesting to note, in light of Miskito and Cuna adaptations,
that interior mountain groups such as the Guaymí of western Panama
and the Talamanca tribes of southeast Costa Rica, which heretofore
have engaged in less constant and less intensive economic activity with
the "outside world," consider virilocality as proper and evidence
either virilocal residence or a mixed pattern of uxorilocal-virilocal-
neolocal residence (Stone 1962: 28–29; Young 1971: 124–140). The
prediction also might be ventured that as Hispanic associations increase the stronger matrilocal traditions of the Miskito and Cuna will
better enable these groups to maintain distinctive social and linguistic
identities, while the Talamanca and Guaymí will lose their traditional
cultural practices and identities more quickly and become absorbed
into the Hispanic rural sector.

Much depends, of course, on the degree of pressure to acculturate to Hispanic practices. To date, such potential agents of change as
government schools and governmentally affiliated village political organizations have been only briefly established and have proved rela-

tively ineffectual (but see Stout 1947: 91). If and when such institutions become more significant and the Caribbean hinterland is more effectively coordinated with the national structure of the Central American republics, greater changes may be expected among all native peoples still resident in the central highlands and Caribbean lowland frontiers.

The essays in this volume provide detailed consideration of a number of points mentioned here and of related topics. As William Duncan Strong noted years ago, "between the southern borders of the Maya in Honduras and the highland territories of the Chibcha in Columbia [*sic*] is a region rich in scientific potentialities for the anthropologist" (1940: 377). This book begins to explore that potential.

Notes

1. For a more detailed statement on the various definitions of "Middle America," see West and Augelli 1966: 1, 5*n*.

2. It is also noteworthy in this context that the distance separating the Basin of Mexico and western Panama (about 1300 miles "as the crow flies") is almost exactly the same as that between the Basin and southern Arizona, where Mesoamerican outposts and influence are well known. Although the factors and conditions were not entirely comparable, the presence of Mesoamericans in lower Central America should not be surprising.

3. Judging from Mesoamerica, long-distance trading systems seem to have been particularly sensitive to European contact and disappeared very quickly after Spanish conquest. Cf. Chapman 1957: 130.

4. It should be noted here that there is no evidence that matrilineal lineages ever existed among the native peoples of Panama in either the pre-Columbian or the colonial era. Concerning residence patterns, the terms "virilocal" and "uxorilocal" are used to indicate the marital residence practices of individuals, while "patrilocal" and "matrilocal" describe patterns characteristic of society in general.

References

Adams, Richard N., 1967. *The Second Sowing.* San Francisco: Chandler.

Augelli, John P., 1962. The rimland-mainland concept of culture area in Middle America. *Annals of the Association of American Geographers,* 52: 119–129.

Bancroft, Hubert Howe, 1886. *The Works of Hubert Howe Bancroft, Vol. 7: History of Central America (Vol. 2: 1530–1800).* San Francisco: History Company.

Baudez, Claude F., 1963. Cultural development in lower Central America. In

B. Meggers and C. Evans, eds., *Aboriginal Cultural Development in Latin America*. Smithsonian Institution Miscellaneous Collection 146. Washington, D.C.

Chamberlain, Robert S., 1966. *The Conquest and Colonization of Honduras, 1502–1550*. New York: Octagon Books.

Chapman, Anne, 1957. Port of trade enclaves in Aztec and Maya civilizations. In K. Polanyi, C. M. Arensberg, and H. W. Pearson, eds., *Trade and Market in the Early Empires*. Glencoe, Ill.: Free Press.

Coe, Michael, 1962. Costa Rican archaeology and Mesoamerica. *Southwestern Journal of Anthropology*, 18: 170–183.

Floyd, Troy S., 1967. *The Anglo-Spanish Struggle for Mosquitia*. Albuquerque: University of New Mexico Press.

Haring, C. H., 1910. *The Buccaneers in the West Indies in the XVII Century*. London: Methuen.

Hay, C. L., et al., 1940. *The Maya and Their Neighbors*. New York: Appleton-Century.

Helms, Mary W., 1969. The cultural ecology of a colonial tribe. *Ethnology*, 8: 76–84.

———, 1970. Matrilocality, social solidarity, and culture contact: three case histories. *Southwestern Journal of Anthropology*, 26: 197–212.

———, 1971. *Asang: Adaptations to Culture Contact in a Miskito Community*. Gainesville: University of Florida Press.

———, in press. Negro or Indian: the changing identity of a frontier population. In A. M. Pescatello, ed., *The African Diaspora*. Westport, Conn.: Greenwood Press.

———, n.d.a. Domestic organization in eastern Central America: the Cuna, Miskito, and Black Carib compared. Unpublished manuscript.

———, n.d.b. Quest for power. Unpublished manuscript.

Karnes, Thomas L., 1961. *The Failure of Union: Central America 1824–1960*. Chapel Hill: University of North Carolina Press.

Kepner, C. D., 1936. *Social Aspects of the Banana Industry*. New York: Columbia University Press.

Kepner, C. D., and J. H. Soothill, 1935. *The Banana Empire*. New York: Vanguard Press.

Kidder, Alfred, II, 1940. South American penetrations in Middle America. In C. L. Hay et al., *The Maya and Their Neighbors*. New York: Appleton-Century.

Kirchhoff, Paul, 1952. Mesoamerica: its geographic limits, ethnic composition and cultural characteristics. In Sol Tax et al., *Heritage of Conquest*. Glencoe, Ill.: Free Press.

Lothrop, Samuel K., 1926. *Pottery of Costa Rica and Nicaragua*, Vol. 1. New York: Heye Foundation.

———, 1940. South America as seen from Middle America. In C. L. Hay et al., *The Maya and Their Neighbors*. New York: Appleton-Century.

———, 1942. The Sigua: southernmost Aztec outpost. In *Proceedings of the Eighth American Scientific Congress*, Vol. 2. Washington, D.C.: Department of State.

———, 1952. *Metals from the Cenote of Sacrifice, Chichen Itza, Yucatan*. Peabody Museum Memoirs, Vol. 10. Cambridge, Mass.

————, 1955. Jade and string sawing in northeastern Costa Rica. *American Antiquity,* 21: 43–51.

————, 1966. Archaeology of lower Central America. In R. Wauchope, ed., *Handbook of Middle American Indians,* Vol. 4. Austin: University of Texas Press.

MacLeod, Murdo J., 1973. *Spanish Central America.* Berkeley: University of California Press.

Meggers, Betty J., 1972. *Prehistoric America.* Chicago: Aldine.

Munro, Dana G., 1967. *The Five Republics of Central America.* New York: Russell and Russell.

Myers, Thomas, 1973. Formative period interaction spheres in the Intermediate Area. Paper presented at the Ninth International Congress of Anthropological and Ethnological Sciences, Chicago.

Naylor, Robert, 1960. The British role in Central America prior to the Clayton-Bulwer Treaty of 1850. *Hispanic American Historical Review,* 40: 361–382.

Nietschmann, Bernard, 1973. *Between Land and Water.* New York: Seminar Press.

Nordenskiöld, Erland, 1938. *An Historical and Ethnographical Survey of the Cuna Indians,* S. Henry Wassén, ed. Comparative Ethnographical Studies, No. 10. Göteborg, Sweden: Etnografiska Museet.

Palerm, Angel, and Eric R. Wolf, 1960. Ecological potential and cultural development in Mesoamerica. In *Studies in Human Ecology.* Pan American Union Social Science Monographs, III. Washington, D.C.

Pendergast, D. M., 1970. Tumbaga object from the Early Classic period, found at Altun Ha, British Honduras (Belize). *Science,* 168: 116–118.

Reichel-Dolmatoff, Gerardo, 1965. *Colombia.* New York: Praeger.

Rouse, Irving, 1962. The Intermediate Area, Amazonia, and the Caribbean Area. In R. J. Braidwood and G. R. Willey, eds., *Courses Toward Urban Life.* Viking Fund Publications in Anthropology, No. 32. New York.

Sanders, William T., and Barbara J. Price, 1968. *Mesoamerica.* New York: Random House.

Sauer, Carl O., 1966. *The Early Spanish Main.* Berkeley: University of California Press.

Solnick, Bruce B., 1970. *The West Indies and Central America to 1898.* New York: Knopf.

Stanger, F. M., 1932. National origins in Central America. *Hispanic American Historical Review,* 12: 18–45.

Stein, Stanley J., and Barbara H. Stein, 1970. *The Colonial Heritage of Latin America.* New York: Oxford University Press.

Stone, Doris, 1962. *The Talamancan Tribes of Costa Rica.* Peabody Museum Papers, Vol. XLIII, No. 2. Cambridge, Mass.

————, 1972. *Pre-Columbian Man Finds Central America.* Cambridge, Mass.: Peabody Museum.

Stone, Doris, and Carlos Balser, 1965. Incised slate disks from the Atlantic watershed of Costa Rica. *American Antiquity,* 30: 310–329.

Stout, David B., 1947. *San Blas Cuna Acculturation: An Introduction.* Viking Fund Publications in Anthropology, No. 9. New York: Wenner-Gren Foundation for Anthropological Research.

Strong, William Duncan, 1940. Anthropological problems in Central America. In C. L. Hay et al., *The Maya and Their Neighbors.* New York: Appleton-Century.

Tax, Sol, et al., 1952. *Heritage of Conquest.* Glencoe, Ill.: Free Press.

Wauchope, R., ed., 1964–. *Handbook of Middle American Indians.* Austin: University of Texas Press.

West, Robert C., and John P. Augelli, 1966. *Middle America: Its Lands and Peoples.* Englewood Cliffs, N.J.: Prentice-Hall.

Willey, Gordon R., 1966. New World archaeology in 1965. In *Proceedings of the American Philosophical Society,* Vol. 110. Philadelphia.

————, 1971. *An Introduction to American Archaeology, Vol. 2: South America.* Englewood Cliffs, N.J.: Prentice-Hall.

Willey, Gordon R., and Philip Phillips, 1958. *Method and Theory in American Archaeology.* Chicago: University of Chicago Press.

Wilson, C. M., 1947. *Empire in Green and Gold.* New York: Holt.

Wolf, Eric R., 1959. *Sons of the Shaking Earth.* Chicago: University of Chicago Press.

Woodward, Ralph Lee, Jr., 1965. Economic and social origins of the Guatemalan political parties (1773–1823). *Hispanic American Historical Review,* 45: 544–566.

Wyman, Walker D., and Clifton B. Kroeber, eds., 1957. *The Frontier in Perspective.* Madison: University of Wisconsin Press.

Young, Philip D., 1971. *Ngawbe.* Urbana: University of Illinois Press.

Part One

PRE-COLUMBIAN THEMES

Competition, Power, and Succession
to Office in Pre-Columbian Panama

MARY W. HELMS

In the early sixteenth century the indigenous Panamanian chiefdoms were composed of two status levels: elites and commoners. The elites included those born to high status, known as sacos, *and warriors or* çabras, *frequently commoners who had achieved social advancement and recognition as lesser elites for their lifetime by virtue of prowess in battle. The social order also included slaves, captives of war, who served as bearers and personal servants of the elites. Above all others was the* quevi *or high chief. Elaborate forms of respect and sumptuary displays were accorded the* quevi, *including travel by litter, the right to wear fine ornaments, large and well-provisioned household compounds, and elaborate funeral rites with sacrifice of retainers. The members of society paid no regular chiefly tribute to the* quevi, *but they were expected to provide whatever services he required for warfare, fishing, planting of his fields, and house building.*

The territory controlled by many of these chiefs included strips of land and river valleys stretching from the central cordillera that runs the length of the isthmus to the Caribbean Sea or to the Pacific coast. (In some cases two polities divided the territory, one settled in lowland and coastal regions, the other in the interior highlands.) The individual lands and villages of a quevi's *territory were in the charge of* çabras *who apparently were directed in turn by* sacos, *who may have served somewhat as "district administrators" for the* quevi.

Although the structure of society as described here appears stable, within the established order a considerable degree of competition and challenge seems to have existed, particularly among the quevis *and* sacos. *In chiefdoms in general it is incumbent upon chiefs to give constant evidence of their abilities to perform their chiefly functions, for he who lacks ability or loses his control of chiefly activities for whatever reason finds many rivals ready to challenge his*

power and position. The following essay analyzes the problem of chiefly succes-
sion to office in Panama from this perspective of competition, interpreting a
statement by Oviedo concerning the strategy followed by the incumbent ruling
line when direct patrilineal succession to the office of chief was broken. The
analysis focuses particularly on the role of high-born women as validators of
chiefly legitimacy.

In the early sixteenth century, at the time of the Spanish Conquest, the mountainous, ecologically diverse Isthmus of Panama contained more than three dozen rank societies or chiefdoms. Unfortunately, we know little about the structure and function of these societies, for after a generation of initial exploration and harsh exploitation many of the Spanish conquistadors who first described Castilla del Oro (as they called the isthmus) were drawn away to the more fabulous wealth of Mexico and Peru, leaving Panama a depopulated and ravaged hinterland (Sauer 1966).

Anthropologists as well (with a few notable exceptions) have given less than full attention to what limited documentary evidence is available; they have preferred, like the conquistadors, to explore the richer and more rewarding sources available for Mesoamerican and Central Andean studies. Consequently, while our understanding of the nature of Panamanian chiefdoms probably will never be fully satisfactory, it remains even more limited than it need be.

By way of exemplifying both the problems presented by limited primary data and the insights that nonetheless can be gleaned from this imperfect ethnohistoric material, I offer here an analysis of the data relating to procedures for succession to chiefly office in pre-Columbian Panama (early sixteenth century). The primary data are contained in a brief, seemingly somewhat confused, and ambiguous description of succession rules by Oviedo:

> The eldest son succeeds his father, and if there are no sons, the oldest daughter becomes the heir and is married to her leading vassal. But if the oldest son is survived by daughters and not sons, the daughters do not become his heirs, but the sons of the second daughter, because they know definitely that she is of their family. Just as my sister's son most certainly is my nephew, and the son or daughter of my brother may be doubted to be his own [1959: 31].

In this passage[1] Oviedo is providing us with the possible moves in the strategy for succession without specifying many of the underlying rules. Consequently, anthropologists have foregone attempts at interpretation except to note, as Stout and Lothrop have, that the key to understanding this passage is contained in the final sentence, which stresses paternity (Lothrop 1937: 26*n;* Stout 1947: 79). This is a reasonable conclusion, particularly since Oviedo provides additional information indicating that the question of paternity among the elites was not entirely academic:

> For the most part these women are virtuous, but there are some, especially high-born ladies, who give themselves to any man who wants them, saying that noble and high-born women should never refuse to grant anything requested of them. Only low-born women refuse [1959: 31].

I believe we can offer additional interpretations which take account of the whole of Oviedo's statement and which reduce the seeming ambiguities by revealing some of the underlying rules for chiefly succession in Panama. However, as a preliminary step we must arrive at some understanding of the overall level of stratification and the attendant dynamics of chiefly status, power, and authority in Panamanian rank societies of the early sixteenth century.

We immediately encounter difficulties in probing this question, since ethnohistoric materials are deficient on many aspects of chiefdom structure and function. But it should be possible to gain some notion of the general operations of Panamanian chiefs and chiefdoms by comparing the available data with studies of chiefdoms in Polynesia, where information is more abundant and where detailed studies of structure and function have been possible. In so doing, we must assume, of course, that a measure of regularity and predictability exists with respect to the general cultural processes responsible for the existence of rank societies and for their basic structural and functional characteristics (cf. Service 1971: Chapter 5; Fried 1967: Chapter 4).

In his volume *Social Stratification in Polynesia* Marshall Sahlins has grouped the societies of Polynesia into three broad categories—I, II (subdivided into IIa and IIb), and III—indicating levels of complexity of stratification in terms of such social, economic, and political criteria as number of status levels, extent and nature of chiefly control of production, and degree of elaboration of sumptuary distinctions for chiefs (1958: 11–12). If the ethnohistoric data on Panamanian chiefdoms are compared with Sahlins' criteria, most Panamanian societies appear to fit the middle range of chiefdoms (Sahlins' group II). No Panamanian chiefdoms were as structurally complex as Hawaii, Tonga, Samoa, or Tahiti (group I) or as loosely structured as atoll societies like Pukapuka, Ontong Java, and Tokelau (group III). Instead, the level of stratification characteristic of Panamanian rank societies appears to correlate best with that of such chiefdoms as Mangareva, Mangaia, Easter Island, the Marquesas, and Tikopia. (For descriptions of Panamanian customs at the time of the Spanish conquest, see Oviedo 1959; Andagoya 1865; Anderson 1914; Sauer 1966; Romoli 1953; and Lothrop 1937.)

Approaching Polynesian materials from another perspective, Irving Goldman (1970) has investigated the nature of chiefly power and has compared and analyzed Polynesian status systems, emphasizing particularly the dynamics of competition for power in rank societies. Goldman groups Polynesian societies into three categories—Traditional, Open, and Stratified—based on variations in the form and operation of the status systems by which power is expressed (1970: 20–24). Unfortunately, the available documents contain even less primary data concerning the expression of power in Panama and the operation of Panamanian status systems than they present on indices of stratification pertinent to Sahlins' classification. Therefore the placement of Panamanian chiefdoms in Goldman's scheme must be determined by indirect means. This can be done by comparing Goldman's classification of Polynesian societies with that of Sahlins, as in Table 1. In general, Sahlins' group I correlates rather well with Goldman's Stratified form of status system, while the societies composing Sahlins' group III are contained in Goldman's Traditional category. Many of the chiefdoms relegated by Sahlins to his group II, where Panamanian data also fit best, are placed by Goldman in the Open category. Since the correlations between the classifications seem to be strong, let us consider the Panamanian status systems as broadly comparable to Goldman's Open system.

For the purposes of this discussion, the most significant feature of the Open status system is the particularly intense status rivalry characteristic of the Polynesian societies in this category. (It should be noted that Goldman feels that the differences between Open and Traditional societies are of degree and do not represent a sharp distinction between the two categories; see 1970: 21.) Among the Open Polynesian chiefdoms traditional genealogical principles for succession to chiefly office, whereby succession was directed and legitimized by the high power, honor, and sanctity of the line of first-born (and descendants of lines of first-born), were modified by overt secular competitions for chiefly power and authority. In other words, while a genealogically valid line of first-born and descendants of first-born

Table 1   The Classifications of Sahlins and
Goldman Compared

Sahlins	Goldman
Group I	Stratified
Hawaii	Hawaiian Islands
Tonga	Tonga
Tahiti	Society Islands
Samoa	(including Tahiti)
	Mangareva
Group II	Open
Mangareva	Samoa
Mangaia	Mangaia
Easter Island	Easter Island
Marquesas	Marquesas
	Niue
	Traditional
Uvea	Uvea
Tikopia	Tikopia
Futuna	Futuna
Group III	
Pukapuka	Pukapuka
Ontong Java	Ontong Java
Tokelau	Tokelau
	Maori
	Manihiki-Rakahanga
	Tongareva

succeeded to chiefly office by virtue of birthright, the incumbents
were frequently forced to meet political and military competition
from others of high status who aspired to chiefly power (Goldman
1970: 24–26).

We can now return to the interpretation of Oviedo's somewhat
tangled statement on succession to chiefly office, bringing with us the
idea that Panamanian chiefs, like their Polynesian counterparts, may
have faced significant competition for power from high-status rivals.
If they did, they must have sought ways to circumvent or reduce this
threat. The key to understanding Oviedo's statement, I suggest, lies
in viewing the several steps he indicates as a "single," technically

patrilineal succession of chiefly office from authorized male to authorized male when direct patrilineal succession is broken.[2] I further submit that Oviedo's description of this "single" succession in terms of several steps or alternatives reflects distinctions recognized by Oviedo and/or his informants between power and status, two related principles that governed not only chiefly legitimacy and efficacy but also the dynamics of status rivalry and competition for chiefly office.

One aspect of chiefly legitimacy that also supports elite rivalry is what we can call *practical authority,* that is, the *socially* recognized element of *effective power* held, if possible, in the Panamanian case by the line of first-born males within the highest-ranking descent group, but potentially attainable by any capable high-status male. Another principle of chiefly legitimacy, however, emphasizes the *personal* element of power deriving from the honor of *high status* accruing to the first-born, regardless of sex, by virtue of the uniqueness of being the first-born in a line of first-borns (Fortes 1973; Goldman 1970: 14–16, 20–24).

In chiefdoms where competition and status rivalry are actively pursued, chiefly legitimacy that can be claimed either by practical authority or by personal status allows a measure of flexibility: the chiefly line may maneuver to protect its position and maintain its control at times of stress. Conversely, emphasis on one or the other of these principles of chiefly legitimacy may provide a contender with fuel for his challenge.

The Panamanian data as recorded by Oviedo become comprehensible in these terms. Oviedo indicates that the normal procedure for succession to chiefly office was direct patrilineal succession, whereby the eldest son succeeded his father. The son presumably held office by virtue of the socially recognized authority accruing to the line of first-born males in the highest-ranking descent group so long as they were acceptably competent in the performance of their duties (Figure 1, Step 1).

If the direct patrilineal line was broken by a lack of sons, then, Oviedo tells us, the oldest daughter became the heir to office and was married to her leading vassal (Figure 1, Step 2). I suggest that the oldest daughter was considered eligible to succeed to high chiefly office by virtue of the legitimacy accorded her through her unique personal status as first-born. However, though she could hold office, she was not socially authorized to *rule,* that is, to exercise effective power in the public sector, since socially or "publicly" significant

Figure 1 Succession to Office in Pre-Columbian Panama, as Described by Oviedo

---

Step 1

"The eldest son succeeds his
father. . . ."

Step 2

". . .if there are no sons,
the oldest daughter [C] becomes
the heir and is married to her
leading vassal."

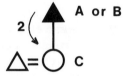

Step 3

"But if the oldest son is survived
by daughters [C] and not sons, the
daughters do not become his heirs,
but the sons [D] of the second
daughter [E], because they know
definitely that she is of their
family. Just as my sister's son
most certainly is my nephew, and
the son or daughter of my brother
may be doubted to be his own."

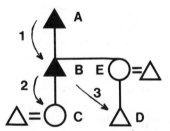

---

power resided in males. It is likely that her husband was expected to act as regent in this respect. Since authority of this sort must be held by someone of high status, she was required to marry her highest-ranking male subject. Her own high personal status by birth-right preserved the formal claim of her descent group to the line of legitimate rule; presumably no one else, including her husband, stood higher in personal rank. (Kathleen Romoli indicates that in the chiefdom of Chape a woman held the chiefly office while a brother served as a sort of "regent-prime minister" [1953: 165]. In this example, if true, the brother was presumably not a first-born male.)

The tenuousness of this claim to office via high personal status—a characteristic of Open societies in Polynesia (Goldman 1970: 22)—is expressed by the final step in Oviedo's report: the son not of the oldest, incumbent daughter but of a "second daughter" is designated heir to the chiefly office (Figure 1, Step 3). To be sure, Oviedo himself indicates that this line of succession is established by virtue of another characteristic of personal status: the link with the ruling descent group provided the son by virtue of the fact of his birth to a female of the group. His mother's identity, regardless of the paternity, indisputably establishes his genealogical relatedness to the ruling descent group, a vital criterion for chiefship. This point is particularly significant in light of Oviedo's statement regarding the sexual generosities of some elite women, but legitimacy accorded by the fact of birth is a universal characteristic which can be found wherever genealogical ties are socially important. With respect to its significance in Panama, it is interesting to note that Andagoya's narrative gives additional evidence for the importance of the fact of birth as a legitimizing principle in Panamanian society: "They married one wife and they held a festival on the day of the wedding. . . . *The sons of this woman* were those who inherited the lordship or house." Other women were taken as concubines, but their children did not inherit (Andagoya 1865: 13; my emphasis).

The importance of the legitimacy provided by the mother also explains why the chiefly office was first settled on a daughter of the deceased chief and not given to his younger brother. The children of a younger brother could not be unreservedly considered genealogical members of the ruling descent group, for there was no sure guarantee that the children were biologically his (especially if Panamanian women were as uninhibited as Oviedo has indicated). In Oviedo's words, "Just as my sister's son most certainly is my nephew, *and the son or daughter of my brother may be doubted to be his own*" (1959: 31; my emphasis). Since this factor of doubt could be used by rival claimants to the chiefship, the emphasis on legitimacy via the fact of birth becomes even more understandable.

The obvious question that now emerges, however, concerns why succession to chiefly office, as validated by the personal status of birth to a woman of the descent group, should be denied to the son of the oldest daughter (she of highest personal descent-group status) and be given instead to the son of the "second daughter," which I interpret to mean the deceased male chief's sister's son. The line of chiefly succession is settled on this sister's son, I believe, because of the high status and power or practical authority held by the oldest daughter's husband by virtue of his wife's office,[3] and the potential challenge that could be launched at the incumbent ruling line if a son of this man's household became chief. This husband's descent group could logically argue that the descent group containing the patri-line of a male ruler (his legal father or mother's husband, father's father, and so on) becomes the ruling descent group by definition. In other words, if the son of the oldest daughter's household inherited the chiefship, the daughter's husband could claim, through his status as highest-ranking male and his role of father (social if not biological) to the new chief, legitimacy of ruling authority for his descent group on grounds of the principle of patrilineal succession. It was in order to avoid this potential challenge, I believe, that the line of succession was settled on the "second daughter's" son.

We are told nothing regarding any prescribed husband for this second daughter, or sister of the dead chief, but we can assume that he probably would not be the highest-ranking male or in a position to acquire effective power in the manner we have suggested for the oldest daughter's husband. Therefore the personal status of the sister as a highly ranked member of the ruling family, together with the genealogical legitimacy accorded to her son by her descent group, would be likely to outweigh any claim to power by her husband's descent group. With the accession to office of a son of this sister, "patrilineal" succession within the ruling descent group is re-established.

By way of conclusion, I should like to consider briefly the significance of this interpretation for our understanding of post-Conquest adaptations by indigenous societies of lower Central America. Regardless of the details of the analysis, some of which admittedly remain speculative, the data definitely indicate that, if the regular line of patrilineal succession to chiefly office was broken, recourse was had to women's personal status as a validating link with the descent group. Ethnographic investigations during the twentieth century have documented the continued, perhaps increased, significance of women's roles in maintaining social identity and solidarity among certain indigenous societies of Panama, most notably the San Blas Cuna (see Torres de Ianello 1957). It seems quite likely that the current importance of women's roles and positions, and of matrilocal residence, reflects an adaptation to the effects of the Conquest, when regular conditions of life were drastically changed. The data presented in this paper suggest that when regular proceedings were disrupted, "emergency" conditions prompted a reliance upon the solidarity and social continuity provided by the line of women. In centuries succeeding the grave upsets of the Conquest, I suggest, this "emergency" procedure (which also proved highly adaptive in an economic context; see Helms 1970) became the norm for the San Blas Cuna, presenting us with the strongly matri-oriented society reported by ethnographers today.

Notes

1. Also found in Oviedo's *Historia general y natural de las Indias* (Madrid, 1851–1855), t. III, lib. XXIX, cap. XXVII, p. 133. Lothrop presents a broadly acceptable paraphrase of this material which, however, should be compared with the original to avoid misinterpretations (1937: 26).

2. Patrilineal inheritance of chiefly office should not be understood to imply that patrilineages were basic social groups. The term "descent group" is used in this chapter to refer to Panamanian kinship groups larger than the family for which we have no evidence regarding lineality as an organizing principle.

3. The oldest daughter's husband's social or public power may have included access to and the right to distribute material goods, a source of chiefly power in and of itself.

References

Andagoya, Pascual de, 1865. *Narrative of the Proceedings of Pedrarias Davila in the Provinces of Tierra Firme.* . . . Trans. and ed. Clements R. Markham. London: The Hakluyt Society.

Anderson, C. L. G., 1914. *Old Panama and Castilla del Oro.* Boston: Page.

Fortes, Meyer, 1973. The problem of the first-born. Lecture presented to the Chicago Anthropological Society in Chicago, Illinois, on November 16, 1973.

Fried, Morton H., 1967. *The Evolution of Political Society.* New York: Random House.

Goldman, Irving, 1970. *Ancient Polynesian Society.* Chicago: University of Chicago Press.

Helms, Mary W., 1970. Matrilocality, social solidarity, and culture contact: three case histories. *Southwestern Journal of Anthropology,* 26: 197–212.

Lothrop, Samuel, 1937. *Cocle: An Archaeological Study of Central Panama. Part I.* Peabody Museum Memoirs, Vol. 7. Cambridge, Mass.

Oviedo, Gonzalo Fernandez de, 1959. *Natural History of the West Indies.* Trans. and ed. Sterling Stoudemire. Chapel Hill: University of North Carolina Press.

Romoli, Kathleen, 1953. *Balboa of Darien.* Garden City, N.Y.: Dolphin.

Sahlins, Marshall, 1958. *Social Stratification in Polynesia.* Seattle: University of Washington Press.

Sauer, Carl O., 1966. *The Early Spanish Main.* Berkeley: University of California Press.

Service, Elman R., 1971. *Primitive Social Organization.* 2d ed. New York: Random House.

Stout, David B., 1947. *San Blas Cuna Acculturation: An Introduction.* Viking Fund Publications in Anthropology, No. 9. New York: Wenner-Gren Foundation for Anthropological Research.

Torres de Ianello, Reina, 1957. *La Mujer Cuna de Panama.* Mexico City: Instituto Indigenista Interamericano.

The Expression of Harmony and Discord in a Guaymí Ritual: The Symbolic Meaning of Some Aspects of the *Balsería*

PHILIP D. YOUNG

The balsería *or* krun, *the stick game of the Guaymí of western Panama described and interpreted in the following essay by Philip Young, almost surely was played in some form by pre-Columbian Panamanians. Unfortunately, as Young notes, the earliest account of* krun *dates from the seventeenth century, a hundred years after contact. Nonetheless, a number of features characteristic of* krun *as reported by post-Conquest observers and Young's twentieth-century informants seem quite compatible with certain aspects of the pre-Columbian chiefdoms of Panama.*

In the preceding chapter it was argued that the Panamanian chiefdoms were characterized by a significant degree of status rivalry and elite competition. It was also pointed out in the headnote to that paper that it was incumbent upon a chief to perform his duties in a capable manner. It therefore follows that a successful chief was also one who could outperform his competitors, and who gave constant evidence of this efficaciousness. The ethnohistoric and archaeological data suggest that Panamanian rulers gave overt indications of their chiefly abilities by elaborate feasting, warfare with neighboring groups, and long-distance trade. These three areas of chiefly activity in turn would have provided the means by which the ultimate in chiefly competence could be demonstrated: the ability to attract and hold the allegiance of a large core of followers—relatives, friends, and especially warriors—by generous distribution of food, trade goods, and loot won in battle.

In discussing his informants' memories of krun, *Young notes that the two principals involved, the host and his* edabáli *or ritual partner, must each have a sizeable band of supporters on whom to rely for support. A successful* krun *provides public recognition for the host or sponsor as the most important man in the area. Young emphasizes particularly the strong theme of competition and of controlled expression of aggression in* krun *activities, as attempts are made to surpass competitors with gifts of food and drink. The author further notes references in the literature to periods of trade following* krun, *and suggests that in pre-Columbian times* krun *provided a period of truce between warring factions during which trade and exchange of goods could take place.*

It seems quite possible that during the pre-Columbian era a ritual game comparable to krun *provided a mechanism by which rival chiefs could overtly display their power by demonstrating their strong bands of supporters, the abundant resources under their control, and their generosity with food and drink. The ritual game itself would also have allowed expression of chiefly challenges, competitions, and hostilities in a controlled situation, reducing the possibility of a socially disruptive escalation of hostilities. The opportunity for trade and exchange that accompanied the ritual, moreover, would have made the meeting an important economic event.*

The krun *as it was described to Young by twentieth-century informants may represent the enactment by what is now an egalitarian society of a ritual that once served mainly the needs of the elite. It is unfortunate that we do not have more data concerning the pre-Columbian ritual and the changes that must have occurred as* krun *was adapted to the needs of post-Conquest Guaymí society.*

The more than 40,000 Chibchan-speaking Guaymí presently occupy an area of approximately 2500 square miles in the mountainous portions of the three westernmost provinces of the Republic of Panama: Veraguas, Chiriquí, and Bocas del Toro. Formerly their territory was more extensive (see Young 1971: 8–10). They live in small dispersed hamlets, practice subsistence agriculture using slash-and-burn techniques, raise small numbers of cattle and other domestic animals, and supplement their diet by engaging in a limited amount of hunting and fishing. They have been in contact with and influenced by European-derived cultures since the time of the Spanish Conquest in the early 1500s. Since the early 1930s the frequency and intensity of contact with the outside world have accelerated and culture change has proceeded at a more rapid rate than previously. Today many Guaymí supplement their subsistence activities by engaging in temporary wage labor on Panamanian cattle ranches and on banana and coffee plantations.[1]

The *krun* (in Spanish, *balsería*) or stick game of the Guaymí has fascinated both scholars and laymen for many years. Yet a review of the literature yields neither a satisfying description of the game itself nor any clear interpretation of the significance of *krun* within the context of Guaymí society. This chapter attempts to remedy the situation in part by providing an ideal-type description of the sequence of activities associated with *krun* and an interpretation of some aspects of the game as ritual.

The earliest account of *krun* known to me is that of Fray Adrian de Ufeldre (1682) who lived among the Guaymí on the Caribbean side of the isthmus between 1622 and 1637. In many respects Fray Adrian's account is more detailed, and to my mind more accurate, than later accounts. While Fray Adrian in several places reveals his disdain for "ye beastly customs of ye savage," his description does agree in several respects with the twentieth-century version of *krun*. There is no way at present, of course, of determining the extent to which the events of *krun* and their meaning for the Guaymí have changed from the seventeenth to the twentieth century. Fray Antonio de la Rocha (1682), who succeeded Fray Adrian in western Panama in 1637 when the latter had to abandon the mission, provides a brief description of a stick game among the Doraces and Zuries, two now-extinct groups related to the Guaymí. This game appears to have been similar to the Guaymí *krun*.

Other accounts that I am aware of, in chronological order, are those of Fray Blas José Franco (1882), who visited the Guaymí at the end of the eighteenth century; A. L. Pinart (1885), who visited the Río Cricamola region of Bocas del Toro in 1883 and who seems to have excerpted parts of his description of *krun* from Franco; Ephraim Alphonse (1956), a Wesleyan Methodist missionary who lived among the Guaymí of the Valiente Peninsula for about twenty years in the early 1900s but who apparently never attempted to do a systematic study of *krun* (or for that matter of other aspects of Guaymí culture); and Peggy Poor (1956), a journalist-adventuress who witnessed part of a *krun* along the Río Cricamola and whose article, entitled "You Bet Your Wife," which appeared in *Natural History* magazine has contributed to the general misunderstanding of what *krun* is all about. Finally, the few comments on *krun* by Frederick Johnson (1948) are perhaps best viewed as interpretation in search of a description.

An analysis, even partial, of the symbolic meaning of aspects of the Guaymí *krun* must overcome several problems. Among the most prominent are these: (1) the game is for the most part no longer held; (2) most current students of the area, including myself, never witnessed *krun;* (3) the published accounts are incomplete and of questionable reliability with regard to both description and interpretation; and (4) the published accounts are virtually devoid of discussion of symbolic meaning, either exegetical, operational, or positional.[2] I have had to rely on accounts provided by informants from memory and their rather sparse comments on exegetical meaning. This chapter, then, is salvage ethnography of a peculiar kind. Nevertheless, I feel it is worthwhile to set forth an account of *krun* and to provide interpretive commentary.

Additional eyewitness accounts of *krun* are unlikely to be obtained. With the rapid spread, beginning in 1961, of the reformative nativistic Mama Chi religion (Young 1971: 212–224) and its doctrine prohibiting both *krun* and *chichería* (a ritual drinking party), *krun* ceased to be held and has not been resumed, at least not on the grand scale of the past. However, in 1972 I received a report that in the area around Peña Blanca in the district of Tolé small neighborhood *krun* were being held. I was unable to substantiate this report, but have little reason to doubt the man (a Guaymí) who provided the information.

With the recent waning of the Mama Chi movement and the sporadic resumption of *chicherías,* the memories of some of my close friends among the Guaymí were refreshed and they were able to provide additional data on *krun* that I had not been able to obtain in either 1964–65 or 1970. During *chicherías* the *edabáli* or ritual-opponent relationship (explained below) is of central importance; it is also quite a prominent feature of *krun.* Some of this new material supplements my earlier account (Young 1971: 204–212) and some of it points up errors in my earlier description of the sequence of activities.

Previous Interpretations

Previous expressions of what is important in *krun* are basically of two kinds. One makes wagering a central theme; the other is the agricultural ritual hypothesis. Aside from the fact that both of these suggested explanations appear to be entirely without foundation (the Guaymí explicitly denied the validity of both), they do not represent analysis of the symbolic meaning of the ritual. I shall not be concerned in this brief chapter to provide a detailed critique of these explanations, but some comment does seem in order.

The first of these explanations, widely believed in Panama, mentioned by Johnson (1948: 251), and asserted by Peggy Poor (1956), is that the chief purpose of *krun* was to wager wives and sometimes property (Johnson 1948) on the outcome of the stick throwing. This explanation, which must be the result of rumor or of untrained or uninformed observation, deserves little credence even as description (my informants consistently denied such reports), much less as explanation, analysis, or interpretation. On this point one of my Guaymí friends commented: "There are people who say that we play for women and land, but that is a story, nothing more. We play to play, that's all." Numerous other Guaymí from San Félix District, Chiriquí Province, also insisted that wives were not wagered on the outcome of the stick throwing, but some did point out that women sometimes left with men other than those with whom they arrived. This was said to be due to preference, not to the outcome of wagers. It is this fact which leads me to suspect that what has been reported as wife wagering at *balserías* in the Río Cricamola region of Bocas del Toro represents some misinterpretation of what was actually taking place.

The second explanation, more insidious than the first because it seems to be generally believed by scholars, is that *krun* was a ritual connected in some significant way with the agricultural cycle. This may be considered as a superficial attempt at explanation in terms of social purpose. There are two variants of this belief. One is that *krun* is somehow intimately related to the harvest of the peach palm (*Guilielma gasipaes*) fruit. This interpretation apparently is based on the fact, first reported by Fray Adrian de Ufeldre (1682), that *krun* took place—at least in some parts of the Guaymí territory—at the time of the peach palm harvest, and it has been strengthened by reports that rituals similar to *krun* also occur at the time of the peach palm harvest among some northern South American groups. In my earlier account of *krun* (Young 1971: 204–212) I have argued that the coincidence of a ritual with an event in the agricultural cycle does not in and of itself serve as proof that the ritual is an agricultural ritual. I wish to expand briefly on this, with specific reference to the relationship between *krun* and the peach palm harvest.

In the Guaymí area the peach palm is less important as a source of food and *chicha*[3] on the Pacific slopes than on the Caribbean. While *krun* apparently did take place at or near the time of the peach palm harvest on the Caribbean slopes, this also happens to be the driest time of the year in an area with no true dry season. *Krun* always took place during the dry season on the Pacific slopes, usually after the felling of the trees on new swidden plots and before planting began. Thus it would seem that the time of occurrence of *krun* may have been related more closely to weather conditions than to the peach palm harvest. This is certainly not too difficult to understand, for it would have been a rather soggy ritual otherwise. It is likely that another reason for holding *krun* at the time of the peach palm harvest on the northern (Caribbean) slopes was simply that the event required substantial quantities of *chicha* and the peach palm fruit served as an admirable source of raw material, the corn supply for this purpose being generally less plentiful on the northern than on the southern slopes.

The second variant of the belief that *krun* is an agricultural ritual derives from Johnson's (1948: 250) statement that *krun* "is connected with agriculture, particularly the planting of crops, but no clear statement of the details has yet been obtained." I would submit that no clear statement of these details is likely to be obtained because the premise is false. Numerous Guaymí on a variety of occasions made explicit statements to me that *krun* was neither a planting nor a harvest ritual and that it was not connected in a significant way to events in the agricultural cycle (that is, for them it was devoid of this type of meaning). The fact that they still retain and celebrate a ritual which they explicitly recognize as an agricultural ritual adds much credibility to their statements about *krun*.

If the importance of *krun* to the Guaymí is neither that of an agricultural ritual nor that of an opportunity to wager wives and other property, what then is its significance? This I shall discuss after presenting a condensed, ideal-type description of the sequence of activities of *krun*.

An Ideal Description

To my knowledge, no detailed descriptions of *actual* sequences of events during *krun* exist. Since by the time I conducted my first ethnographic field research among the Guaymí the opportunity to witness the large-scale *krun* of times past had vanished with the rise and spread of the Mama Chi movement, I was confined to recording events as the memories of my informants construed them. In recollections of specific *krun*, the descriptions, undoubtedly lacking in minute detail and to some extent in accuracy, were certainly not ideal-type descriptions—nor did my subjects intend them to be. One such description is presented in my book (Young 1971: 207–209). None will be presented here. Rather, what I will provide here is a formal or ideal sequence, a reflection of what the knowledgeable Guaymí believe ought to be the progress of the ritual. The formal elements of the ritual will provide the substance upon which an interpretation of the symbolic meaning of *krun* may be based.

PRELIMINARY ARRANGEMENTS

The preliminary arrangements involve the extension of an invitation by a man in one hamlet and its acceptance by a man from another. The Guaymí say that host and guest should be from areas at a considerable distance from one another, though no minimal distance is specified, probably because the idiom is one of kinship rather than of geographic space. That is, the success of the event depends upon both host and guest having a sizeable following of participants, the majority of whom are relatives (the Guaymí reckon kinship cognatically rather than lineally), and this is more likely to be the case when overlap of kinship relations between host and guest is minimized by geographic distance. Both the sponsor and his principal guest have to be sure of the support of the people in their respective areas—relatives, neighbors, friends—before they can enter into the arrangement. Acceptance of the invitation places host and guest in the *edabáli* or ritual-opponent relationship, of which more will be said later. Many of the supporters of each of the principals will also have *edabáli* relationships with members of the opposite group; these will be activated during *krun*. The Guaymí render *edabáli* in Spanish as *contrario* (opponent, rival), a fact which itself says something of their view of the relationship. I shall use the terms "host" and "guest" to denote the two roles in the *edabáli* relationship.[4]

Upon receiving word of acceptance of the invitation, the sponsor and his group begin to make the necessary preparations, including the cutting of the balsa sticks, called *balsas,* which are left to dry for several weeks. At a later date, but still several weeks before the event, the sponsor (*kububu*) sends two emissaries to inform his ritual opponent of the time and place for the *krun*. These messengers carry knotted strings (*ki igwa*) to mark off the remaining days. On their journey they periodically blow conch shells; thus their arrival as well as the nature of their mission is well advertised. The emissaries are wined and dined, mostly wined, with a continuous proffering of *chicha* which they have to accept until they become thoroughly inebriated. On the following day they are given gifts of food for the return journey. The principal guest then repeats the procedure by sending two emissaries to the sponsor, who convey the guest's acceptance of the arrangements. Word of the agreement is never sent back with the sponsor's emissaries, because the formalities of ritual take precedence over efficiency. Additional procedures are followed if, for some reason, there is a change in the agreed-upon day.

As the time for *krun* draws near, the sponsor and his supporters prepare enormous quantities of drink and food, and the honored guest and his group make preparations for their journey to the designated location. The *krun* itself is described by the Guaymí as a four-day event, as explained in the following sections.

THE WAITING TIME

Allowing a sufficient number of travel days to arrive at the specified location on the appointed day, the party of the honored guest sets out amid the blowing of conch shells and much other noisemaking. When the guest and his followers are less than a day's travel from the designated site they encounter the sponsor's emissaries, who have been sent with *chicha* and food to insure that the honored guest does not suffer thirst or hunger. When his *edabáli* is near, the sponsor himself goes out to greet him with *chicha* and informs his ritual opponent that he and his group must spend the night where they are (which is always near the field in which the *krun* is to take place). This afternoon and night are known as *ni kede bïda,* the waiting time.

THE WATCHING TIME

On the following morning the first full day of *krun* begins. This is called *nw)de n)ere,* the watching time. The sponsor leads his *edabáli* by the hand to the place that has been set aside for him at the end of the playing field opposite that of the sponsor and his group. Other men of the sponsor's side who have established *edabáli* relationships with members of the invited side likewise seek out their ritual opponents, lead them to the places arranged for them, and give them *chicha.*[5] Then each host takes his *edabáli* to his own camp, where he gives him a continuous supply of *chicha* and occasionally some food until, ideally, the guest collapses, thoroughly inebriated. Hosts must drink with their *edabáli,* and relatives on both sides also participate. Consequently, most men (and many women) get ritually drunk in the course of the festivities. The ritual drinking continues throughout the night, accompanied by much singing and dancing in which both men and women participate.

Fights are not infrequent and in this way insults are responded to and grudges settled, but even here the procedure is ritualized. Two men fight facing each other until one is knocked to the ground. His opponent then helps him up and leads him off to offer him *chicha*. *Edabáli* never physically fight with each other. During the watching time the balsa sticks (also called *krun*) are guarded by the sponsor's selected men so that no one may use them in a fight.

THE PLAYING TIME

On the third day, *krun n)ere*, the playing time, all begin preparations before dawn, painting their faces and putting on their finest and fanciest clothing and ornamentation. Men bedeck themselves with beaded collars, fancy feathered headpieces, and stuffed animal skins.[6] Many of the guests have by now found opponents for the stick throwing.

Every man has a special name which he uses at *krun*. He is never known by his ordinary name at this event, and even his special name is not supposed to be offered directly. When his *edabáli* in the course of giving him *chicha* asks his name, he tells his ritual opponent to ask his brothers. A person is known only by his special name to those of the opposing side during *krun*, even though several individuals of the opposing side may well know him by his given name.

Eight men from each side, chosen respectively by the sponsor and his *edabáli* for their valor and skill, formally commence the game. The eight guests race across the *llano*, a large, flat, grassy area, amid much noise announcing their arrival, and take up positions opposite their opponents with their backs turned. The eight hosts are positioned in a line, four on either side of the rack holding the *balsas*. Two *balsas* with their ends wrapped in leaves are taken from the rack by the two men of the host side closest to it and, at a signal from the sponsor, they throw at their opposites who return the throws. The sticks should strike only the calf of the leg; a blow anywhere else is considered a foul and cause for indignation and anger. The *balsas* are then thrown by the next set of men and so on until they have been thrown by each of the eight men on each side (see Figure 1). This sequence is repeated four times and then all drink *chicha* for a few minutes. The sequence of four throws per man is then repeated, after which the stick throwing is open to all who wish to participate. The sponsor and his *edabáli* (according to statements collected in 1972) never throw the sticks at each other, though they can and do participate in the stick throwing with other opponents. Ideally, no one engages in stick

Figure 1 The formal commencement of the stick throwing. The throwing sequence shown here is repeated four times, followed by an interlude for *chicha* drinking, and then is repeated four more times.

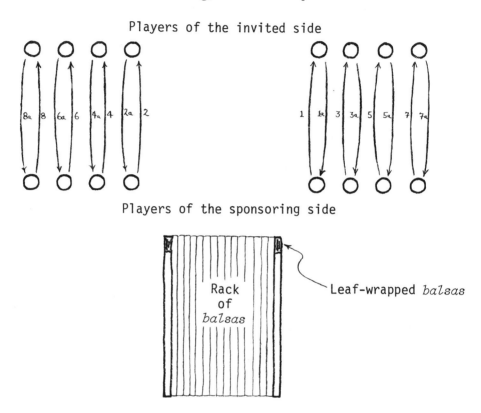

throwing with his own ritual opponent. *Edabáli* take care to point out brothers and sons to one another because ideally they are not supposed to engage in stick throwing even with close relatives of their ritual opponents.

The throwing contests continue all day until about six in the evening, when the sponsor gives the order to collect the *balsas* and the game is officially over. In the evening the men of the invited side, with family and relatives, are again wined and dined by their *edabáli*. All then retire to their own camping places to sleep and await the morning.

THE DEPARTING TIME

On the morning of the fourth day, known as *krun hondrin n)ere,* the departing time, the sponsor again leads his *edabáli* by the hand to his camp and offers him *chicha* that has been reserved for the departure. Each man of the sponsoring side does likewise with his own *edabáli*. All but a small amount of the remaining *chicha* is consumed at this time. Following this, the sponsor and other men of the sponsoring side lead their ritual opponents to the edge of the camping area and give them substantial quantities of both cooked and uncooked food (meat, rice, beans, green bananas, etc.) to sustain them and their relatives on the journey home. A small portion of the cooked food is returned by the ritual opponent to his host. The recipients of these generous prestations are required to share with their less fortunate companions, that is, those who on this occasion did not find *edabáli*. The remaining *chicha* is consumed and the guests depart.

Such is the idealized version of *krun* as told to me by men who in the past had been participants.

The Meaning of Krun

Several aspects of *krun* are symbolic of general features and patterns of behavior and emotion in Guaymí society. The ritual as a whole displays both the ideal of harmonious relationships and the inevitable discord that characterize Guaymí life. But beyond this gross level of symbolic representation it is possible to examine the symbolic meaning-content of *krun* as ritual.

Turner (1967:19) defines ritual as "prescribed formal behavior for occasions not given over to technological routine, having reference to beliefs in mystical beings or powers." The Guaymí *krun,* so far as I was able to ascertain, bears no reference to beliefs in mystical beings, but there is reference to beliefs in mystical powers if we define mystical power loosely. *Krun* may thus be considered a ritual in Turner's sense. It fits more squarely, however, within Firth's (1951: 222) somewhat broader definition of ritual "as a kind of patterned activity oriented towards control of human affairs, primarily symbolic in character with a non-empirical referent, and as a rule socially sanctioned."

It is possible that in pre-Columbian times *krun* served to provide a period of truce within a ritual context respected by both sides, so that warring factions might come together to trade or for some other purpose. In the early-seventeenth-century account of Fray Adrian, mention is made of a fair, held after the stick throwing, at which people exchanged their goods and wares. (Of course, Fray Adrian also informs us that the stick throwing itself lasted two days rather than one [*dos dias duraba este confusion*] and this is apparently erroneous.) While a comparison of *krun* with the ritual feasting of the Yanomamö groups of northern South America makes the truce-trade hypothesis seem reasonable, direct historical evidence to support this contention is lacking. *Krun*, moreover, has not served this purpose in the recent past, for it has been some time since the Guaymí have been at war with each other or with anyone else. It should also be kept in mind that while the twentieth-century description of *krun* is similar in many ways to the three-centuries-old description of Fray Adrian, the purpose and meaning of the ritual may have shifted considerably.

After brief examination of the significance of "four," I shall comment only on the use of alter-names, the *edabáli* relationship, *chicha*, and food prestations in order to illustrate the interplay of harmony and discord in the ritual of *krun*.

THE NUMBER FOUR

The events of *krun* take place mainly during two full days of activities, yet the Guaymí describe it as a four-day event. Eight men of the host group and eight of the invited group align themselves four to the left and four to the right of the rack holding the *balsas* and each throws the *balsa* four times; this is followed by an interlude and a repetition of the four throws by each man. And ideally two opposing groups celebrate *krun* four times before seeking other opponents. The number four is also conspicuous in other areas of Guaymí life and belief. It represents to them correctness, properness, and pattern fulfillment, and this is important in their description of what should take place during *krun*. The symbolic meaning of "four" makes it clear that it serves as a rhetorical device to indicate proper and correct procedure in the ritual of *krun* rather than what might actually have taken place at any particular *krun*.

THE ALTER-NAME

The Guaymí explanation for the use of special names during *krun* is simply that one should conceal his identity during this ritual. Implicit in the explanation is the idea that during *krun* a man is not himself; he assumes a different and separate identity, an alter ego. This would serve to confine any consequences of his interaction with others to the context of the ritual itself. With regard to the stick-throwing contests and the hand-to-hand fighting, it would mean that injuries sustained or embarrassment and ridicule suffered could not legitimately be avenged outside the ritual context of *krun*. The alter-name is thus a device to prevent antagonism generated at *krun* from escalating into a feud in everyday life. It does not, of course, prevent a man in his alter-identity from attempting to settle a grudge he has against another by engaging the other's alter in fighting or stick throwing. In fact, this apparently was a frequent occurrence. The use of alter-names by *edabáli* obviates the reciprocation of drink and food until alter-identities are again assumed within a ritual context.

EDABÁLI

The stick throwing during *krun* can be viewed as a manifestation of aggression under carefully controlled conditions in a ritually structured context, and thus as a symbolic expression of discord. The *edabáli* relationship cannot be so easily interpreted, for it is Janus-faced. Any interpretation of the *edabáli* relationship must recognize that on a general sociological level of meaning both harmony and discord are symbolically represented in the behavioral acts that are a prescribed part of this relationship.

Once established, the *edabáli* relationship continues for life. Any man may have several *edabáli* and thereby any woman may have several as well, for when men enter into this relationship their respective wives are also said to stand in the *edabáli* relationship to each other. At a *chichería edabáli* always have seconds who must also be *edabáli* to each other; this was not mentioned in connection with descriptions of *balsería* but I assume it to be the case there as well.

That *edabáli* never throw the *balsas* at each other does not mean that the relationship contains no expression of rivalry. Though "feasting partner" or "ritual drinking partner" is descriptive of the surface-level, or manifest, interaction between *edabáli,* I believe it is significant that the Guaymí without exception render *edabáli* in Spanish as *contrario* (opponent, antagonist, competitor, rival). It is thus evident that the relationship for the Guaymí involves rivalry played out in a ritual context. A man offers drink to his *edabáli* but he must also drink with him. As the Guaymí express it, a man attempts to "knock down" his opponent with drink and avoid being knocked down himself. *Edabáli* fight with drink. During this ritual drinking exchange, a man's relatives may—in fact are expected to—help by drinking some of the *chicha* offered him. The activity symbolizes both aggression and the support one expects from kinsmen in the face of aggression. But even more is involved.

Giving of food and drink forms the basis of friendly relationships in Guaymí society. As part of a reciprocal relationship this is proper and productive of harmony. But giving within the context of the *edabáli* relationship is so exaggerated that reciprocity becomes difficult, if not impossible, and thus it assumes the proportions of an antisocial act symbolic of aggression. Such exaggerated giving is permissible only within a ritual context where it is kept under strict control by the formal requirements of the ritual. Therefore interaction between *edabáli* symbolizes both the hospitality that is customary in Guaymí society and the hostility which is always potentially lurking beneath the surface in social relations.

CHICHA

The Guaymí say that they cannot work effectively if they do not have *chicha*, for it is *chicha* that gives them strength. *Chicha* may thus be viewed as symbolic of strength. During *krun* every man receives a super-injection of this strength. In everyday life offering *chicha* also serves as an expression of genuine hospitality. During *krun chicha* drinking takes place in a context of ritual opposition so that, while it is symbolic of hospitality on the one hand, it is symbolic of aggression on the other.

FOOD PRESTATIONS

When the hosts give their *edabáli* food for the journey home, the guests give back a small quantity. The Guaymí say that this is traditional, meaning required. They believe that this will insure that there will continue to be food in a host's house and that the *edabáli* will come there to eat again. They say it is not necessary that the host accept this return offering. The gesture is what is considered important. Thus the exchange symbolizes the enduring nature of the *edabáli* relationship and the pattern of reciprocity that is inherent in it.

The general pattern of sharing during the ritual of *krun* (and during *chichería*) mirrors that which occurs in mundane social relations. Within the ritual context, however, there is displacement of mundane patterns to the level of symbolic meaning. Illustrative is the fact that *edabáli* do not exchange or formally request food from one another in everyday life as one does from relatives, though *edabáli* may be relatives, nor do those who are not *edabáli* exchange drink and food in the ritual context.

Conclusions

Gluckman distinguishes four kinds of ritual: "[1] Magical action, connected with the use of substances acting by mystical powers... ; [2] religious action, the cult of the ancestors, also acting in this way; [3] substantive or constitutive ritual, which *expressed* [my italics] or altered social relationships by reference to mystical notions, and of which *rites de passage* were typical; and [4] factitive ritual, which increased the productivity or strength, or purified or protected, or in other ways increased the material well-being of a group" (1962: 23). The Guaymí *krun* is a constitutive ritual within this framework.

Krun as a ritual event symbolizes in numerous ways, blatant and subtle, both the harmony and the discord that are omnipresent in the ordinary life of the Guaymí. My first inclination was to view this ritual as symbolic primarily of aggression, but closer attention to the details of activities in the ritual made it clear that *krun* must be seen as a symbolic representation of both friendliness and hostility. Symbolic aggression is most explicit in the stick-throwing and fighting activities. The dual symbolism of harmony and discord is best seen in the *edabáli* relationship. *Krun* also serves to provide the sponsor with public recognition as the most important man in his area (Young 1971: 211), and in this limited sense it serves as a *rite de passage*. For the society at large, however, it is more an expression of, than an alteration of, social relationships.

In this brief chapter I have not attempted to explore the relationship between the *krun* of the Guaymí and the ritual feasting found among various indigenous peoples in northern South America. Suffice it to say that *krun* is part of the northern South America ritual pattern and that it shares with the rituals of aggression in that area the following features: physical blows exchanged between opponents, use of verbal insults, exchange (giving) of *chicha* and ceremonial food, and potential for escalation. There is some evidence that the possibility always existed at *krun* for fights of a semi-ritual nature to escalate into killings and feuds. Thus there are similarities here to the dueling feasts of northern South American groups described by Chagnon (1968) and earlier commented on by Pinart (1887) and Termer (1919). But the Guaymí attempted to prevent such happenings by restraining (in stocks in post-Conquest times) anyone who desired to escalate matters beyond a simple hand fight. It can also be suggested that the mechanism of alter-names may have served as a deterrent to carrying hostilities beyond the ritual context of *krun*.

Gluckman's (1962: 41) statement that "a man is not at one time a friend and at another an enemy, but always both a friend and an enemy" is an apt way of stating the central theme that seems to pervade the symbolism in the Guaymí ritual of *krun*.

Acknowledgments

The research upon which this chapter is based was supported by the National Institutes of Mental Health and the University of Oregon, for which I am grateful. I also wish to express my gratitude to John Bort, Don Messerschmidt, Richard Smith, Chuck Smythe, Ted Stern, and Henry Wassén, who provided comments on the earlier version of this essay. I assume responsibility for any errors of fact or interpretation that remain in the present version.

Notes

1. For a detailed account of the economic and social organization of the western Guaymí, see Young 1971.
2. Turner (1967: 50–51) defines these three levels of meaning as follows: exegetical meaning is equivalent to indigenous interpretation; operational meaning is what people do with ritual symbols, as opposed to what they say about them; and positional meaning involves a symbol's "relationship to other symbols in a totality, a *Gestalt,* whose elements acquire their significance from the system as a whole."
3. *Chicha* is a fermented beverage which can be made from a wide variety of fruits, grains, or tubers. *Chicha* made of corn is the most common variety among the Guaymí.
4. The Guaymí also use the term *edabáli* in a more general sense to refer to all members of the opposing side during *krun*.
5. The composition of camps on each side follows the ideal of virilocality (Young 1971: 132).
6. If earlier accounts may be believed, the stuffed animal skins which men wear on their backs during *krun* are believed by the Guaymí to impart the power (and the characteristics?) of the animal to the wearer.

References

Alphonse, Ephraim S., 1956. *Guaymí Grammar and Dictionary with Some Ethnological Notes.* Bureau of American Ethnology, Bulletin No. 162. Washington, D.C.: Government Printing Office.

Chagnon, Napoleon A., 1968. *Yanomamö: The Fierce People.* New York: Holt, Rinehart and Winston.

Firth, Raymond, 1951. *Elements of Social Organization.* Boston: Beacon Press.

Franco, Fray Blas José, 1882. *Noticias de los indios del departamento de Veraguas y vocabulario de los lenguas guaymi, norteno, sabanero, y dorasque.* Coleccion de linguistica y etnografia americanas, Vol. 4. San Francisco: A. L. Pinart.

Gluckman, Max, 1962. Les rites de passage. In M. Gluckman, ed., *Essays on the Ritual of Social Relations.* Manchester: Manchester University Press.

Johnson, Frederick, 1948. Caribbean lowland tribes: the Talamanca division. In J. H. Steward, ed., *Handbook of South American Indians,* Vol. 4. Bureau of American Ethnology, Bulletin No. 143. Washington, D.C.: Government Printing Office.

Pinart, A. L., 1885. Chiriqui. Bocas del Toro—Valle Miranda. *Bulletin de la Société de Géographie,* Ser. 7, Vol. 16: 433–453.

———, 1887. Les Indiens de l'état de Panama. *Revue d'ethnographie,* 6 (1): 33–56; 6 (2): 117–132.

Poor, Peggy, 1956. You bet your wife. *Natural History,* 65: 308–313.

Rocha, Fray Antonio de la, 1682. Del Padre Fray Antonio de la Rocha y de la conversion de los indios de la Provincia de San Salvador de Austria de los Doraces y Zuries en el Reino de Panama, hecha por su grande celo. *Tesoros verdaderos de las Indias,* Vol. 3. Rome: N. A. Tunassio.

Termer, Franz, 1919. Ein Beitrag sur religiosen und kulturellen Leben der Guaimiindianer im 16. Jahrhundert. *Korrespondenz-Blatt der deutschen Gesellschaft für Anthropologie, Ethnologie und Urgeschichte,* 50: 9–12, 52–55.

Turner, Victor, 1967. *The Forest of Symbols: Aspects of Ndembu Ritual.* Ithaca, N.Y.: Cornell University Press.

Ufeldre, Fray Adrian de, 1682. Conquista de la Provincia del Guaymí. . . . In *Tesoros verdaderos de las Indias,* Vol. 3. Rome: N. A. Tunassio.

Young, Philip D., 1971. *Ngawbe: Tradition and Change Among the Western Guaymí of Panama.* Urbana: University of Illinois Press.

Mesoamerican Influences Among Talamanca and Western Guaymí Indians

LAURA LAURENCICH MINELLI

In pre-Columbian lower Central America, where many aspects of culture patterns and processes remain uncertain, the question of Mesoamerican influences is particularly elusive. Nonetheless, the sum of available evidence leaves little doubt that diffusion occurred and that more direct contacts took place. In the following essay Laura Minelli presents social, mythological, and linguistic evidence of Mesoamerican influences among indigenous peoples of western Panama and southeastern Costa Rica.

Among other things, Minelli discusses the frequent use of the surname "Montezuma" among headmen or caciques of post-Conquest Western Guaymí groups, noting that use of this name and supposed descent from the Mexica emperor Moctezuma are offered as evidence of the individual's legitimate right to rule. This situation suggests parallels with the use of the term "Toltec" among post-Classic Mesoamericans. In the economic and political realignments following the collapse of the Toltec state, numerous small ruling lineages struggling to assert claims of supremacy in the central Mexican and Guatemalan highlands claimed Toltec ancestry in order to emphasize and validate their right to rule. (A comparable situation existed during the Toltec era at Chichén Itzá in Yucatán.) Some of these ruling lines may have held legitimate claim to Toltec ancestry, but many others simply seem to have used the term because of its connotation of "rightful, legitimate ruler" (cf. Wolf 1959: 123–126). Possibly the illustrious name of Montezuma served a comparable purpose among western Panamanian and southeastern Costa Rican "men of importance" competing for the right to claim power and authority after the Spanish Conquest had upset society and disrupted traditional methods of legitimizing the right to rule.

The term has continued to be used to the present day as a title signifying "rightful ruler," as Minelli indicates.

Minelli further suggests that the Guaymí caciques using this name are connected in some manner with direct Mexica (Aztec) domination in the region, possibly emanating from the colony of Mesoamericans known as Sigua whi h was located near the Sixaola river basin of southeastern Costa Rica. Whether or not these de facto ties with the Mexica state originally existed is a point for further study, but is not crucial for understanding the political usefulness of the term "Montezuma" for native caciques.

Minelli also recounts portions of a mythological song of the Guaymí concerning two heroes, the wise chief Deko and Ciri Klave, a strong and wily newcomer who tricked and defeated Deko and destroyed him. A second myth describes Ulikron, a culture hero who traveled far and wide, promising one day to return. These two accounts again suggest parallels with Toltec materials, in this case the famous Náhuatl legend of the confrontation between Topiltzin-Quetzalcoatl and the fierce and treacherous Tezcatlipoca at Tula, the Toltec capital just north of the Basin of Mexico. Topiltzin-Quetzalcoatl was defeated and forced to flee the land. In some versions the hero died and rose to the sky to become the morning star, while in other accounts Topiltzin-Quetzalcoatl sailed away to the east, promising someday to return (cf. Coe 1962: 134–138).

Let us also note a few additional culture traits, not discussed by Minelli, which have been mentioned in the literature as possibly indicative of Mesoamerican contacts or influence in lower Central America. Stone (1956), for example, has tentatively proposed that the rather limited use of maize by Talamanca peoples indicates a late pre-Columbian introduction of the grain by Mesoamerican colonists. Sauer finds evidence in the ethnohistoric data relating to sixteenth-century Panama for such Mesoamerican traits as quilted cotton battle armor, the turkey, and a ball game; all these items are indicated among peoples of the Pacific coast of western Panama, a region where, in Sauer's opinion, changes in customs and language suggest the mixing of Mesoamerican and Intermediate Area cultural traditions (1966: 270–272, 275).

The existence of an Aztec colony in southeastern Costa Rica from the sixteenth to the seventeenth centuries, first in the vicinity of the Sixaola river basin and later on the island of Tojar, has been known to Americanists for a century. Thomas and Swanton (1911) stated that although its presence has been denied by some scholars the historical evidence leaves little doubt of the colony's existence. As recently as 1942 Lothrop exhaustively examined the documentary evidence and concluded that, together with other isolated Aztec colonies in Central America, the Sigua[1]

> represent a consistent scheme of expansion, conceived by Emperor Ahuitzotl and continued under his successor, Montezuma II. Had not the Spaniards arrived, it seems quite possible that the Aztec in course of time might have conquered or made tributary most of Central America.... At any rate, the Sigua represent the process of expansion of a strong military state, arrested before it had attained maturity [1942: 114–115].

In this chapter I shall examine probable traces left by these colonists among Western Guaymí and Talamanca Indians, who presently live in the neighborhood of the ancient Sigua colony. In addition to these relatively recent traces, there are some more nebulous traits which suggest a more ancient contact of the Western Guaymí and Talamanca with Mesoamerican peoples.

Western Guaymí and Talamanca Indians

Let me begin with a brief survey of cultural characteristics found among the Western Guaymí and the Talamanca Indians. The observations I report here concerning the Western Guaymí derive mainly from my field work in 1966 and 1972 among a Western Guaymí group living near the southeastern border of Costa Rica in the vicinity of San Vito de Java.[2] They call themselves Mǫ̧ve, and in this chapter I shall restrict the use of this name to the Costa Rican group.[3] In analyzing my data I have relied for comparison mainly on the work of Alphonse (1956) among the Guaymí of the Valiente Peninsula and to a lesser extent on the work of other authors listed in the bibliography. Following Stone (1962: 6) I consider "Talamanca" as "an all-inclusive word for the Bribri and the Cabecares," among whom I conducted field research in 1963 on the Pacific slope and in 1972 on the Atlantic. The observations I report here come mainly from my field notes and the work of Stone (1962) and Gabb (1875).

The Western Guaymí and Talamanca Indians belong to the Intermediate culture area which extends from the southern frontier of Mesoamerica to the Colombian and Ecuadorian Andes and the western Venezuelan Andes. As might be expected from its geographical position between Mesoamerica and Peru, the Intermediate Area's cultural development has been complex. Currents of influence from both Mesoamerica and Peru can be recognized, and the cultures of the Intermediate Area in turn influenced those of the other two areas (Willey 1971: 254–255).

The Western Guaymí and the Talamanca share a common cultural substratum that seems oriented mostly to the south. As stated by Stone (1958: 678), "The non Mexican non Maya peoples of Central America demonstrate a sameness in their culture pattern that points toward the southern hemisphere." Torres de Arauz (1964: 271–272) has already pointed out some traits shared by the Talamanca and Guaymí cultures, such as round dwellings, the absence of villages, the use of bark cloth, the *sukia* (or shaman), and the woman's being considered tabu during childbirth and her first menstruation. In addition, some traits of the girl's puberty ceremony are common to both cultures, as is polygyny (limited to four wives among the Talamanca and unlimited among the Guaymí); we might also find some likenesses in the social systems, Torres said, "if we knew a bit more about the actual situation among the Guaymí" ("si supieramos un poco mas cerca de su situacion real entre los Guaymí"). Twelve years have passed since Torres wrote those words, yet we cannot draw firm conclusions on the matter because the results of research have been extremely variable. According to Young (1970: 86), the system of kinship terminology among Ngawbe is cognatic and residence is virilocal, while among Mōұve Bozzoli and I noticed a preferred matrilineal system with matrilocal residence that is rather similar to that of the Talamanca (Bozzoli de Wille 1974; Laurencich 1974a: 372).

To the list of traits common to Talamanca and Guaymí I would add the use of the *quipu* (knotted string) for counting and sending messages (as I observed during my most recent field work among Guaymí and Talamanca); the fact that both languages belong to the Chibchan stock; the practice of face painting, still common to both female and male Mōұve (Laurencich 1974a: 377) and once frequent among Talamanca (Stone 1962: 20); the use of secret personal names indicating plants and animals (perhaps identifiable with the spirit animal protector), once found among Talamanca (Stone 1962: 27) and other Guaymí (see Young's chapter in this volume); the importance of the forest both as a food resource complementing the agricultural diet and as the purported residence of divinities personified by the animals and plants of the forest itself (Laurencich 1974a: 371); fishing, hunting, and agricultural methods and implements; the staple diet of tubers, *pejibayes*, bananas, and *plantanos* and the secondary position of maize which, furthermore, is consumed not as tortillas but mainly as *chicha;* and modes of transportation and of carrying burdens, for instance the use of the frontal tumpline.

Within this common sphere, however, the two cultures are well differentiated from one another. For example, in addition to linguistic differences, the Guaymí practice the *balsería,* as Young has discussed in the previous chapter; in this game they evidence the concept of the "alter ego" by wearing the skin of an animal over their shoulders (Johnson 1948: Plate 45). The Guaymí also practice the *clarido,* chip and file the upper incisors (Laurencich 1974a: 377), and practice some cranial oblique-cylindrical deformation (*ibid.*). None of these customs are found among the Talamanca. Conversely, Talamanca practice secondary burial (Stone 1962: 18–19, 29) and a complex ceremonialism (Laurencich 1974b); they preserve traces of a "theocracy" (*ibid.;* Stone 1962: 41–42); and their medicine men use a secret language (Laurencich 1974b; Stone 1962: 42; Lehmann 1920: 399). I have observed none of these traits among the Guaymí. In addition to these cultural items, it should be noted that the Bribri, Cabécar, and Guaymí display similar physical (phenotypic) characteristics, though specific features serve to distinguish them well (Laurencich 1966, 19-74a, 1974b).

Traces of Mexican-Mesoamerican Influences

Some possible Aztec traits and others more indeterminate that I call Mesoamerican may still be noted among contemporary Western Guaymí and Talamanca peoples. Here I shall briefly summarize these cultural, mythological, and linguistic characteristics, beginning with the use of "Montezuma" as a surname. Montezuma, the *cacique* (leader or headman) of the Mōʉve of Desamparado-Caño Bravo, told me in 1966 that he was a descendant of the Mexican emperor and for this reason claimed that he was rightfully *cacique* of the entire Mōʉve group. The existence of *caciques* or kings named Montezuma or Moctezuma was noted long ago among Western and Eastern Guaymí (Seemann 1853: 173–182; Pinart 1887; Nordenskiöld 1928: 176; Wassén 1952: 277), and I would call attention to the old tradition which links the name of Montezuma, as descendant of the Aztec Montezuma, with the claimed right of *cacicazgo* among the Guaymí. Seemann (1853: 177) pointed out that "king Lora Montezuma . . . pretend[ed] to be a descendent of the Mexican Emperor" and informed Spanish authorities that he was the legitimate lord of the country. This behavior is similar to that displayed by my friend Montezuma in 1966. This so-called "right" may be a trace of some ancient Aztec domination in the Isthmian region, as also suggested by historical documentation (Lothrop 1942: 115). Hence I would consider with Wassén (1952: 279) that the Guaymí *caciques* named Montezuma are somehow connected with the historically attested Aztec colonists (Sigua) in southeastern Costa Rica. This hypothesis may be strengthened by Alphonse's (1956: 44) observation that the word "Montezuma" still reveals the link of the Valiente Guaymí to early Mexican colonists called *deko,* meaning "ancient." Personally I suppose the word *deko* is the Guaymí translation of the Bribri *sigua* and probably refers to the same southernmost Aztec colonists Lothrop calls Sigua (1942). In fact, one of my Mŏųve interpreters told me *deko* means "foreigner" or "stranger," not "ancient" as stated by Alphonse.

Another trace of Mexican influence in the northern Intermediate Area can be found in the mythical song recounted by Alphonse concerning two successive Mexican invasions among the Valiente Guaymí, the first by the wise chief Deko, the second by Ciri Klave, who won the contest between the two and transformed Deko into a stone.

> The Ciri Klave came in a great canoe. His oars were studded with great pearls. His canoe was splendid in the sun, splendid on the water; his slaves that rowed him were splendid in dress, in beads.... The Ciri Klave beat our chief; his arms were stronger; his sense was greater... [Alphonse 1956: 125].

Alphonse also recounts another mythical song about Ulikron, who seems to be a Valiente version of Quetzalcoatl, the great god and culture hero of Mesoamerica, also known as Kukulcán.

> The Ulikron... traveled from the north.... He talked to stout little men, to tall red men, to men in huts, to men in tall houses made of stone.... Yes, the Ulikron passed among them long, long ago and told men to be good, to do good, to love good.... The Ulikron went down to the end of the earth. He went to the far south and talked. He saw the land of gold and the land of great waters... he told men to be good and that he would come again for all good men.... All Indians wait for the "Ulikron" [Alphonse 1956: 125].

In addition to the use of the name "Montezuma" and the evidence of myth, numeral classifiers may give evidence of Mesoamerican influence. Numeral classifiers are present in some languages of the Chibchan stock—for instance, Bribri, Cabécar, Terraba-Tiribi, and Boruca of the Talamanca-Barbacoa group and Guaymí-Dorasque of the "Dorask-Guaymí" group (Rivet and Loukotka 1952: 1113)[4]—while, as far as I know, numeral classifiers are absent from the other Chibchan languages. On the other hand, numeral classifiers seem common to Náhuatl (Molina 1945) and to Mayan languages (Berlin 1968). The numeral classifiers belong to a peculiar (for us) counting system. Before numeral and classifier the enumerated object noun is placed. Before the specific numeral (in Western Guaymí) or after it (in Bribri, Cabécar, Náhuatl, Maya) the classifier affix is placed, indicating the class to which the enumerated object belongs (class of round objects, of elongated ones, of flat ones, etc.). In other words, things are specified not only in terms of quantity but also in terms of other characteristics such as shape. In Mōu̯ve, for example, the same noun, such as *digmá* (banana), may belong to the class of trees, of heaps, of elongated objects, or of flat objects, depending on whether we are counting banana trees, heaps of bananas, detached banana fruits, or leaves of the banana tree. Another example is "house," which is placed in the class of round objects by the Bribri, Cabécar, and Western Guaymí. In Mōu̯ve *hu kua ti* means one house; *hu* is house, *kua* is the round-object classifier, and *ti* means one. The reason for this classification is that traditionally the dwellings had a circular floor plan.

The fact that this numeral system occurs in the above-mentioned northern Chibchan languages may be due to Náhuatl or Mayan influence among these Chibchan peoples. By trading with their Mesoamerican neighbors, they may have absorbed the concept of the numeral system while maintaining their own terms or vocabulary. I have not found any Mayan or Náhuatl influence in Talamanca and Guaymí numerals or in other words connected with the numeral classifier system. It is also possible that the system derives from an ancient pre-Chibchan language common to these regions as well as to Mexican and Mayan ones; or it may have developed in different areas independently.

The use of a vigesimal counting system is also relevant to this discussion. Western Guaymí (Mōu̯ve and Valiente) and Cabécar (but not Bribri) have a vigesimal counting system as do Náhuatl and

Mayan languages. Cabécar is quinarian-vigesimal like Náhuatl while Western Guaymí is decimal-vigesimal like Maya. All have a common vigesimal base (Laurencich 1974b). This fact may be somehow related either to some direct Mayan or Náhuatl influence among these peoples or to the Mesoamerican calendar (both the 260- and the 360-day calendar have a vigesimal base), or it may have developed independently. Personally, I would rather consider it a calendrical influence which was not absorbed by the Bribri, who never had their own priest class. The calendars were prerogatives of the priest class and were used mostly for presaging purposes. According to their legends, the Bribri entered the Talamanca region in the relatively recent past and conquered the Cabécar (Stone 1962: 35). The latter, however, maintained their intellectual and priestly leadership over the Bribri even after being conquered (Stone 1962: 7).

There is also the possibility that codices (presumably Mexican in tradition) existed among the Western Guaymí. This hypothesis is supported by a special numeral classifier, actually used for counting book pages, and by the etymology of the Mōyve word for "book," which literally means "to hold skin" (tóro kuáda ká-ti means one book; tóro means to hold, kuáda is skin, ká is the book-page classifier, and ti means one), as well as by the oral tradition of Ciri Klave, who could read and write (Alphonse 1956: 71). Possibly the term for "book" refers to folded parchment like that found in Mexican codices, where the parchment, folded like an accordion, is held by two tablets or hard leather covers.

Finally, we must consider the sacredness of the number four, which Young's chapter in this volume describes as a characteristic of the Guaymí. Four is also recurrent in Cabécar mythology—for instance, the four wives of Sibu, the creator-god, and the four kinds of cacao—and in the social rules of the Talamanca peoples, where, for example, polygyny is allowed within the limit of four wives (Stone 1962: 65). This emphasis on the concept four might be a derivative of Mesoamerican cosmology, though this is very uncertain.

Conclusions

Some possible Mexican traces still notable among living Western Guaymí Indians, such as the use of Montezuma as a surname and the myths of invasions and of Ulikron, suggest a rather recent contact between Western Guaymí and Mexicans. The latter are probably identifiable as the so-called Sigua Mexican outpost, the existence of which has been historically documented (Lothrop 1942) in southeastern Costa Rica. More nebulous and less certain Mesoamerican traces, including numeral classifiers, the use of a vigesimal counting system and the number four, and perhaps also codices, may suggest some more ancient cultural influence in the northern part of the Intermediate Area. They may also derive from an ancient pre-Chibchan common cultural substratum shared by Mesoamerica and the northern Intermediate Area.

Notes

1. *Sigua* means "stranger" or "foreigner" in the Bribri language.
2. Here I follow Wassén's (1952) division of Guaymí Indians into Western and Eastern groups, a scheme that clarified earlier interpretations. Pinart (1882: 7), quoting Padre Franco, grouped Guaymí into two "nations," Norteños and Savaneros. This old division, while unclear to us, may have been valid at Padre Franco's time, the end of the eighteenth century. The intrusion of Europeans among the Guaymí during the last century may have caused a westward movement of the Norteños, as I found by examining the birthplaces of Mōyve ancestors, and also probably caused an eastward movement of Savaneros.
3. Linguistically the Costa Rican Mōyve and Lehmann's Move are identical. I am also inclined to consider their language either the same as, or a dialectical variant of, that of Young's Ngawbe (1971).
4. In this chapter I deal mainly with Bribri, Cabécar, Mōyve, and Valiente; for the other mentioned languages the reader may consult Lehmann (1920: 172–175).

References

Alphonse, Ephraim S., 1956. *Guaymí Grammar and Dictionary with Some Ethnological Notes.* Bureau of American Ethnology, Bulletin No. 162. Washington, D.C.: Government Printing Office.

Berlin, Brent, 1968. *Tzeltal Numeral Classifiers: A Study in Ethnographic Semantics.* The Hague: Mouton.

Bozzoli de Wille, Maria Eugenia, 1974. Terminologia de Parentesco Guaymí. In *Revista America indigena* (in press).

Coe, Michael, 1962. *Mexico.* New York: Praeger.

Gabb, William, 1875. On the Indian tribes and languages of Costa Rica. In *Proceedings of the American Philosophical Society,* Vol. 14. Philadelphia.

Johnson, Frederick, 1948. Caribbean lowland tribes: the Talamanca Division. In J. H. Steward, ed., *Handbook of South American Indians,* Vol. 4. Bureau of American Ethnology, Bulletin No. 143. Washington, D.C.: Government Printing Office.

Laurencich, Laura, 1966. Notas antropométricas sobre los indios actuales de Boruca, Salitre, Ujarras. In *Actas del XXXVI Congreso Internacional de Americanistas*, Vol. 3. Barcelona.

———, 1974a. Un grupo de indios Guaymí en la region sur de Costa Rica (notas etnograficas, linguisticas, antropológicas). In *Actas del XL Congreso Internacional de Americanistas*, Vol. 2. Rome.

———, 1974b. Osservazioni etnografiche ed antropologiche su di un gruppo di Amerindi Bribri e Cabecar di Costa Rica. *Archivo per l'antropologia e l'etnografia*, 104. Firenze.

Lehmann, Walter, 1920. *Zentral Amerika: die Sprachen Zentral Amerikas in ihren Beziehungen Zueinander sowie zu Sud-Amerika und Mexico*, Teil 1. Berlin: Dietrich Reimer Verlag.

Lothrop, Samuel, 1942. The Sigua: southernmost Aztec outpost. In *Proceedings of the Eighth American Scientific Congress*, Vol. 2. Washington, D.C.: Department of State.

Molina, Alonso de, 1945. Vocabulario en lengua castellana y mexicana. In *Colección de incunables americanos, siglo XVI*, Vol. 4. Madrid: Ediciones Cultura Hispánica. (First published in 1571.)

Nordenskiöld, Erland, 1928. *Indianerna på Panamanäset*. Stockholm: Ahlen and Akerlunds.

Pinart, A. L., 1882. Noticias sobre los indios del Departamento de Veragua y vocabulario de lenguas Guaymi, Norteno, Sabanero y Dorasque. In *Colección de linguistica y etnografia americanas*, Tomo IV. San Francisco.

———, 1887. Les Indiens de l'état de Panama. *Revue d'ethnographie*, 6: 33–56, 117–132.

Rivet, Paul, and C. Loukotka, 1952. Langage de l'Amerique du Sud et des Antilles. In Antoine Meillet and Marcel Cohen, *Les langues du monde*. Paris: Centre Nacional de la Recherche Scientifique.

Sauer, Carl O., 1966. *The Early Spanish Main*. Berkeley: University of California Press.

Seemann, Berthold, 1853. The aborigines of the Isthmus of Panama. *Transactions of the American Ethnological Society*, Vol. III. New York.

Stone, Doris, 1956. Date of maize in Talamanca, Costa Rica: an hypothesis. *Journal de la Société des Américanistes de Paris*, 45: 189–194.

———, 1958. A living pattern of non Maya non Mexican Central American aborigines. In *Miscellanea Paul Rivet, octogenario dicata*. Mexico City: Universidad Nacional Autónoma de México.

———, 1962. *The Talamancan Tribes of Costa Rica*. Papers of the Peabody Museum of Archaeology and Ethnology, Vol. 43, No. 2. Cambridge, Mass.

Thomas, Cyrus, and John Swanton, 1911. *Indian Languages of Mexico and Central America*. Bureau of American Ethnology, Bulletin No. 44. Washington, D.C.: Government Printing Office.

Torres de Arauz, Reina, 1964. Nexos de los Guaymies con los Pueblos Talamanquenos. *Actas del XXXV Congreso Internacional de Americanistas*, Vol. 3. Mexico City.

Wassén, Henry, 1952. Some remarks on the divisions of the Guaymí Indians.

In Sol Tax, ed., *Indian Tribes of Aboriginal America.* Selected Papers of the Twenty-ninth International Congress of Americanists, Vol. 3. Chicago: University of Chicago Press.

Willey, Gordon R., 1971. *An Introduction to American Archaeology,* Vol. 2. Englewood Cliffs, N.J.: Prentice-Hall.

Wolf, Eric R., 1959. *Sons of the Shaking Earth.* Chicago: University of Chicago Press.

Young, Philip, 1970. A structural model of Ngawbe marriage. *Ethnology,* 9: 85–95.

———, 1971. *Ngawbe: Tradition and Change Among the Western Guaymí of Panama.* Urbana: University of Illinois Press.

Tapirs and Manatees: Cosmological Categories and Social Process Among Rama Indians of Eastern Nicaragua

FRANKLIN O. LOVELAND

Analysis of myth and symbolism, not only in terms of inherent structures and context but also as part of the ecological method, is slowly shedding light on basic questions of cultural patterns and processes in Middle and South America (see Furst 1968; Lathrap 1973). In the following essay, using mythological and observational data, Loveland presents an interpretation of the conceptual and processual significance of the tapir and the manatee among the Rama Indians of southeastern Nicaragua, a small group of hunting-fishing-agriculturalists, most of whom now reside on a small cay in Bluefields lagoon.

On the conceptual level Loveland finds the tapir associated with the natural world, noise and disruption, social disorder (via sexuality and affinal relations), and agriculture, while the manatee is symbolic of the cultural world, quiet, social order and solidarity (via communitas*), and resources of the water. On the processual level Loveland illustrates how the manatee hunt and the butchering, distribution, and consumption of manatee meat and by-products provide a ritualized expression of community cooperation and solidarity. The tapir, on the other hand, is accorded no special processual or behavioral significance. In conclusion, Loveland raises the apt question of what relationship might exist between the relative availability of tapir and manatee and the patterns of symbolism among the Rama.*

The analysis of myth and symbolism among eastern Central American lowland groups may help to unravel some of the earlier periods of lower Central American culture history. Adjacent to the Central American Caribbean lowlands are the lowland regions of the Petén and Yucatán to the north and the Orinoco-Amazonian basins to the south. Archaeological and ethnological in-

vestigations of these major lowland areas have generally emphasized ties with adjacent highland blocs of Mesoamerica and the Andean chain, respectively. Few comparisons have been made of the adaptations by Mayan lowland societies and peoples of Amazonia to the tropical conditions common to all. When such investigations are performed, the cultural patterns and processes of eastern Central American lowland groups, which are geographically and perhaps culturally intermediate, may be expected to acquire new significance and interest for anthropologists. In all these tropical lowland regions where archaeologists may face difficult problems of material preservation, analysis of more indirect sources, including myth and symbolism, may notably assist in the reconstruction of pre-Columbian developments (cf. Lathrap 1973). Loveland's findings are of the sort that might be used for this purpose. Contemporary ethnologists may also discover important comparative materials in such sources, for myths often contain rich ethnographic data as well as information relevant to culture history.

It is most interesting to find in this latter respect that Loveland's material may reflect aspects of recent Rama culture history. Possibly the particular processual significance accorded the manatee today reflects adjustments in living patterns caused by the dispersal of Rama peoples from their original homeland in the Río Punta Gorda basin of southeastern Nicaragua and the move to Rama Cay, where the majority of Rama live today. This resettlement occurred during the late eighteenth century in response to depredations by the militant Miskito Indians, who were expanding territorially during the eighteenth and nineteenth centuries at the expense of other indigenous groups. Manatees may have had relatively less processual (though still conceptual) significance prior to this disruption, when subsistence may not have been oriented as heavily to lagoon and ocean fishing and hunting. The disruption of traditional patterns and migration to the cay would not only have facilitated greater utilization of lagoon products but would also have required that new symbols of social solidarity be found, or older ones given greater overt expression, if Rama culture was to continue. This situation may have led the Rama to increase the ritual significance accorded the hunting, distribution, and consumption patterns associated with the manatee.

This chapter represents an attempt to make anthropologists aware of certain basic issues which confront the analyst with regard to conceptual systems in lower Central America. It discusses certain mythemes that have a long and important history in Central and South American cultures and that are important for understanding social behavior in the surviving cultures of lower Central America.

Specifically, this essay will deal with the cosmology of the Rama Indians of eastern Nicaragua regarding two significant animals: the tapir and the manatee. It will become apparent through the analysis of behavioral and historical data as well as of myth that these animals play important symbolic roles in the cosmologies of Central American peoples, particularly the Rama.

The Rama Indians

The Rama reside in four major settlements in the tropical forest along the east coast of Nicaragua; most of them are located on Rama Cay, a small island in Bluefields lagoon where I did my field work.[1] They are one of the northernmost peoples speaking a language of the Chibchan family. The Rama live in a coastal rain forest environment like that of some of the Miskito (Nietschmann 1973), a multiple econiche environment which includes the tropical forest and its rivers, the estuary lagoon, and the Caribbean Sea. Hunting, gathering, and agriculture are the important means of subsistence along the river and in the surrounding forest, while fishing and gathering shellfish, nuts, and seeds are important in the lagoon-ocean environment. Fishing does occur in the riverine environment and farming can occur on the border of the lagoon, but these are exceptions rather than the rule. Conceptually the environments are rather distinct, but the Rama note that during the rainy season the lagoon becomes "sweet" like the river and the riverine fauna replace the ocean fauna which are found in the lagoon during the "dry" season. As I have argued elsewhere (Loveland 1971), the constant alternation of environments is culturally elaborated in Rama cosmology and provides a "contrast model" for all relationships in Rama myth.

As with many other cultures, the Rama are conceptually preoccupied with affinal relationship. The affinal relationship like the environment is in a state of constant flux and is filled with anxiety, which is frequently elaborated upon in myth. The relationship between brothers-in-law (defined in Rama terms) is conceptually an ambiguous one; in various Rama tales the brothers-in-law either kill their sister's husband or are killed by him. The Rama themselves cite cases in which brothers-in-law have disinherited one another from what was legally theirs. Interestingly enough, it is the tapir that symbolizes the sister's husband or the brother-in-law who is killed.

This chapter examines how the Rama symbolically utilize the

tapir to conceptualize the ambiguous affinal relationship and also how the Rama achieve social solidarity processually by utilizing the manatee hunt and feast as a symbol of *communitas* or social integration. To examine these important points we must first note historical accounts of these animals and several myths which will put these animals in their cultural-historical context. Then we will discuss Rama attitudes toward the tapir and manatee as revealed by the behavior and ceremony associated with hunting, butchering, and eating these animals. From this comparison we will discover the conceptual roles of tapir and manatee as metaphors of order and disorder, and of process and structure, in Rama thought.

Historical Accounts of the Tapir and the Manatee

Historically travellers have been struck by the manatee and tapir and the natives' interest in these animals. One need only reflect on Esquemeling's description of the sea cow in his *Buccaneers of America,* originally published in 1684 (1967: 243), or Dampier's description of the manatee in *A New Voyage Round the World,* first published in 1697 (1968: 32). The elaborate descriptions of the animals, their habits and habitat, and the methods of hunting them make us aware of their importance at that time.[2]

The particular contrasts or oddities of the manatee noted by the Indians and the explorers include the following:

1. The manatee, though a water animal, resembles the European land cow. It is warm-blooded like a land animal yet it prefers to live in water.
2. It has no ears (pinna) but only holes which function as ears and three small bones (auditory ossicles) through which sound travels. Nonetheless, it has an extremely keen sense of hearing.
3. The skin of the manatee is very tough. Therefore the harpoon point used in killing manatees is different from the ones used for fish and turtles.
4. In color the meat is like beef but it tastes like pork.
5. The manatee contains a great deal of fat.
6. The manatee migrates in salt water but always returns to fresh water.
7. The meat of the tail and unweaned calf is most esteemed.

The earliest mention of the tapir in the literature is in William Williams' *Mr. Penrose,* originally published in 1815 (1969: 232). Another brief mention of the tapir is to be found in Roberts' 1827 account (1965: 45). The most complete description of the tapir is that by Squier, whose book was first published in 1855 (1965: 165). Bell also mentions the tapir in *Tangweera* (1899). There is much fiction in these early descriptions but they provide us with valuable information on how the Indians and to some extent the explorers viewed the tapir and its contrasts with other animals. The details which are of particular importance to us are:

1. The tapir is nocturnal, in contrast to the manatee which is predominantly diurnal.
2. Unlike the manatee, which wanders or even migrates, the tapir is found in fixed haunts to which it travels by unvarying paths.
3. The tapir is not aggressive but uses its ability to move quickly and to swim to flee potential attackers.
4. The tapir makes a commotion in moving about through the forest, unlike the manatee which is extremely quiet.
5. The tapir, like man, is not afraid of fire, but it is afraid of the jaguar, which along with man is its chief predator.
6. The tapir is a pest, since it feeds on certain domestic crops.
7. Like the Rama, the tapir prefers the riverine forest environment to the savanna or coast.

These observations indicate that the peoples of the Miskito coast have long had an intimate knowledge of the fauna in their environment. Furthermore, the observations or beliefs regarding the manatee and tapir reveal a series of "culturally elaborated" contrasts, as shown in Table 1. We might compare Lévi-Strauss's suggestion that "animals are good to think" (1963: 89).

It is insights such as those in Table 1 that are the basis of the conceptual system associated with the tapir and the manatee, both of which are extremely important in Rama myth. The tapir, in the Rama view, is exactly the opposite of the manatee and this "natural" contrast becomes the basis of the "cultural" contrast. As we shall see, the manatee is associated with culture, society, and order while the tapir is associated with nature, asociality, aculturality, and disorder. The duality of the manatee's habitat (salt and fresh water), its quietness, and its migratory habits make the manatee an excellent animal symbol for the Rama themselves.

Table 1 Contrasts of the Tapir and Manatee, from
Historical Accounts

	Manatee	Tapir
Living habitat	Water	Land
Period of daily activity	Diurnal	Nocturnal
Habits	Quiet and migratory	Noisy and with fixed haunts
Food	Aquatic plants	Domestic plants

Tapir and Manatee Myths

There is a body of Rama and Miskito myths which deals with tapirs
and manatees. Myths have been recorded by Berckenhagen (1894), by
Hamilton (n.d.), and by myself during field work at Rama Cay in
1969–1970. The texts fall into the general category of what Kramer
calls "animal tales," although they do have many features of what he
would call "myths" (1970: 101–102).

Rama and Miskito narratives dealing with manatees and tapirs
fall into two groups: those dealing with the origins of the animals and
those about their activities. The origins of the manatees and tapirs are
described in a myth which was recorded by Hamilton among the
Miskito in the 1920s and by myself among the Rama in 1970. The
myth, in the version I heard, is as follows:

> In the old, old days [creation times] the mountain cow and the manatee
> were one. The mountain cow couldn't stay in the water so they take him
> out. He stayed on land. The next one they put, that is the manatee, now
> in the water and he swim away but I couldn't remember any more.

Hamilton's version reads:

> *Origin of tapir and manatee.* The manatee and tapir were originally
> brothers. The tapir was the older, the manatee the littler. They bet each
> other they could dive across a stream from one bank to the other. The
> older got stuck in the middle, but reached land as a tapir. The other
> struggled across to the far bank; in the water it had changed into a
> manatee [Hamilton n.d.: 14].

The second type of narrative dealing with the activity of these
animals is represented by two stories, one heard in Miskito by

Berckenhagen (1894) and the other a Rama story recorded in English by myself. Both are stories about tapirs. In the Berckenhagen Miskito text a tapir is fooled out of his inheritance of a flute by a howler monkey.[3] In the Rama text a lost woman has a son by a tapir and the tapir is killed by her brothers because he eats their crops. The tapir instructs her to remove and dry his testicles, which will provide the son with an abundance of fish. The woman's brothers make fun of the human-tapir boy because he makes so much noise when he walks, and the boy runs away into the bush to become the tapir we know today. The full text of the Rama narrative is given in the Appendix to this chapter.

Taking both groups of narratives as a whole, it is clear that they develop the theme of social differentiation of consanguineal and affinal relationships. In the first group, in both the Rama and Miskito texts, animals which metaphorically are of the same family become differentiated by virtue of their respective habitats or, in the Miskito narratives, by their ages. In the second group of narratives the Rama tapir is further transformed by his relationship with a human being and her family. In the Miskito myth the tapir loses its flute and the monkey does not reciprocate, while in the Rama myth the tapir feeds freely on his brothers-in-law's crops and does not reciprocate except in his death, when he gives humans fishing magic. Thus in the Rama narrative the tapir symbolizes two potential sources of social disorder—the affinal relationship and the unreciprocated gift. In the Miskito narrative it is inheritance which becomes the source of conflict.[4] In both versions the tapir symbolizes the individual outside of culture and society.

Ceremonial Aspects of the Manatee and Tapir

Social-action systems are crucial for understanding the manatee and tapir in their wider context as "key symbols" (Ortner 1973: 1340) in Rama society. Data gathered on Rama manatee and tapir hunting indicate that these animals are important for subsistence. While fewer tapirs and manatees have been killed in recent years than in the past, they still are animals of great significance in the minds of the Rama. The Rama constantly asked my wife and me if we had tasted manatee meat. Since we had not, they constantly reassured us that if things were good that year a manatee would be killed and we would taste its sweet meat.

The Rama word for manatee is *palpah,* which is the same as the Miskito term. According to Daniel Hartman (personal communication), the animal is probably *Trichechus manatus manatus,* which is found throughout the Caribbean. The Rama believe that the manatee is very intelligent and that it has an acute sense of hearing. Like humans, it dislikes excessive noise and is easily frightened away. Furthermore, a manatee knows whether or not a Rama is "looking him" (hunting him).

Hunting the manatee in Rama land involves the ultimate confrontation between hunter and hunted. Special harpoons with a distinctive style of point are used by specified individuals who are designated as manatee hunters. In 1969–1970 there were eight manatee hunters in all, but only three or four who "looked" (hunted) manatee during that year. In a recent communication from an informant, the author was told that there are now five men who are involved in hunting manatee. Formerly, there was an old woman who was considered to be an excellent manatee striker, but generally nowadays women do not hunt manatee.

Manatee hunters work alone or in pairs. By the time the season of the "big" rains is underway, the lagoon is turning "sweet" and the manatees move out into it. It is during this season, then, that the manatee hunters leave at dawn to hunt the animal. Insofar as could be determined, partnership from other subsistence activities is carried over into manatee hunting. The "striker" always is in the bow of the dory (dugout canoe) while the other partner, the "captain," guides the dory in the direction of the manatee. Since manatees have an extremely keen sense of hearing, both the striker and the captain take care not to make the least bit of noise. The manatee frequently feeds around the river mouth where the current flows out into the lagoon, and the Rama increase their chances of killing a manatee by approaching it against the current, so that the muddy or turbid waters of the estuary impair the animal's vision and sense of smell. However, the danger that the manatee will hear the hunters is always present because sound travels well through water. For this reason the Rama utilize as "magic" the earbone of the manatee to keep the creature from hearing them. The Rama also believe that if a man is sick he cannot hunt manatee because the manatee would smell him. A final key to success in killing a manatee is to keep the paddles from splashing or hitting the side of the boat.

Generally two boats will work a wide area within sight of one another. Some strikers, however, prefer to work alone. Some people prefer to hunt by staying in one place and waiting for the manatees to come to them, while others actively seek the animals out. Once a manatee has been harpooned a conch shell is blown and the other dory will come to help the successful hunter. The manatee may be loaded into the boat if it is small or towed behind if it is large. The manatee is brought directly to Rama Cay to be butchered and is left in the water while the striker decides who will butcher it. The butcher and his helpers are given the ribs of the manatee. Generally the butcher is a consanguineal kinsman of the striker, but in recent years nonkinsmen such as a close friend of the striker, perhaps a neighbor, have been chosen as butchers. The butcher, in turn, chooses the helpers who assist with the butchering and the distribution of the meat and also with keeping the dogs away from the meat. The helpers receive the guts of the manatee and some of the blood, which is thought to be very potent.

The meat must be roasted and eaten immediately or the hunter will not be able to find another manatee. The striker cannot eat any of the butchered meat. However, he does receive the tail, breastplate, and earbones, which (with the exception of the earbones) he redistributes. An average-size manatee provides some 200 pounds of steaks (Nietschmann 1973: 165). When a manatee was killed in 1970 at Rama Cay, each of the thirty-four families on Rama Cay received five pounds of roasted or fried meat. Normally, the remainder is taken to Bluefields, where it is sold. If the striker is a good man, he will use the money to buy cigarettes and coffee which, in turn, he will distribute to all the families on Rama Cay.

The eyes and earbones are removed from the head, as is the brain, and the head is used to make a soup. The fat is also boiled to make soup. If the manatee is female the breasts and vagina are removed to "defuse" the animal sexually. The penis and the testicles of a male manatee are removed. If the female is pregnant the Rama will eat the fetus if it is of good size. They believe it is "hot" meat, since anything associated with pregnant women is humorally categorized as "hot" as opposed to "cold." The manatee skin may be dried to make various objects, including whips to control those who become drunk or angry. The skin is also fed to the dogs and is dried and given to old people to eat in times of scarcity. A calf or newborn infant is a special delicacy. The beginning of the food distribution is announced by a conch-shell horn. The sign of a successful feast of manatee is when everyone is filled up and becomes sick from eating all the rich meat and soup. The cooks are always women; men never serve in this capacity.

After the feast, the striker must return all the bones to the spot where he killed the manatee or he will be unable to find a manatee again. The Rama believe that returning the manatee bones to the lagoon will allow the manatees to become used to people and will insure that there will be more manatees in the future.

Several additional points should be noted:

1. Although in general the striker of a manatee may not eat its meat, this rule does not hold when a man kills his first manatee. Then he is given a special piece of meat from above the heart to insure that he will kill more.
2. After a manatee has been killed the hunters bathe in its blood. This ceremony, which is supposed to help them to keep finding manatees, involves certain interesting ideas regarding conception, since bathing in the blood makes them like fetuses.
3. The manatees are guarded by a large whale which can cause the current to reverse and which will devour anyone who should try to harm the manatees in their home in Tarpon lagoon.
4. The striker holds high status in the community, implicit in the fact that he does not talk about his techniques or charms used in hunting.

It is evident that the manatee serves as a symbol of unity for the Rama Cay community and, furthermore, that the hunting of the manatee and the distribution of its meat to all of the members of the community function as a "ritual of *communitas*" or as an explicit "key paradigm" in Rama culture (see Ortner 1970). The sexual "defusing" of the manatee symbolizes the asexuality which social relations of the *communitas* type necessitate. A second dimension of manatee symbolism is the identification of the manatee with the Rama themselves. The Rama refrain from talking about the location of the manatee while hunting it, or even about hunting charms they carry, because they believe that with its acute sense of hearing the manatee is sure to know what is going on. In this way it is like a human being. Like humans and the jaguar, moreover, the manatee is silent and therefore is on the side of culture. Noise to the Rama is a sign of nature, not culture. The silent or "cultural" manatee contrasts sharply with the "natural" tapir, which makes a tremendous amount of noise when traveling through the bush. One could also argue that the manatee's position as a "key symbol" in Rama culture represents the precedence of water over land resources in the present Rama Cay subsistence system.

The tapir, associated with land and agriculture, is important in Rama myth but ceremonially is not nearly as important as the manatee. This is particularly evident because the Rama attach little symbolic significance to the hunting and killing of tapirs. These activities are not subject to any special rules. The Rama simply enjoy eating tapir meat and say that it is very tasty. Unlike the manatee, which is hunted during the day, tapirs are hunted at night through the use of lights. (As noted above, tapirs are not afraid of fire or lights.) Because the tapir moves along the river banks, almost all hunting for tapirs is done along the rivers and creeks of Rama land. If a tapir is heard in the vicinity, men will seize their guns, follow it by its sound, and kill it. The greatest danger in hunting tapirs, according to the Rama, is that they will charge humans. In addition, if a Rama is in a boat in the river and should encounter a tapir in the water, the tapir can upset the boat and cause a drowning.

The distribution of tapir meat follows the same pattern as for other land animals. The owner of the gun receives one-fourth of the meat, the hunter's companion one-fourth, and the hunter who killed the tapir one-half. Since a tapir is a large animal, it furnishes more meat than most other land animals, and some meat may be sold. It is important to emphasize that a feast is not held.

The Rama utilize the tapir to symbolize human relationships and concerns, but in a distinctly different way from the symbolism of the manatee. The tapir becomes a symbol of conflict and asociality in the context of Rama myth, as we demonstrated above. Likewise, it is a symbol of unrestrained sexuality and predation on domesticated crops. All of these elements of its symbolic character are the antithesis of the symbolism of the manatee. Conceptually and ceremonially, the manatee and the tapir stand in opposition to one another. However, they are linked by the fact that both are potentially important sources of meat today and can feed a large number of people. While the tapir is not the focus of elaborate ritual or of hunting technique, it is a good source of meat and as a game animal may be equivalent to the manatee. It is this aspect of the tapir which overrides its symbolic attributes of disorder and makes it the "brother" of the manatee and the source of fishing magic.

One final question that may be raised concerns why the tapir is conceptually significant in Rama myth, while the manatee becomes a dominant or "key symbol" in the processual frame of Rama culture. Does this reflect a decline in the population of tapirs and a subsequent decline in interest in hunting the tapir? The presence of a large body of tapir tales throughout the Central American and South American culture area would argue against this interpretation, but still the argument may be significant for understanding the symbolism of the tapir and manatee. It is possible that the cosmology of the manatee is only now developing for the Rama and Miskito. (However, it is imperative to keep in mind that manatee hunting has a long history in the Miskito coast area and that other neighboring cultures such as the Warao have some stories about the manatee.[5]) It is also possible that the manatee, which conveys solidarity, is better suited for "acting" than for "thinking" while the tapir, which conveys disorder and conflict, is better "thought" than "acted." This simply means that, in certain cultures, certain animals are weighted differently in the spheres of thought and action. Alternatively one could argue that thought and action may not be separated artificially and that as symbols the two animals refer to different domains of social action. The manatee could be considered a symbol in the secular public domain of ceremony while the tapir is a symbol in the sacred private domain of myth.

It is important to continue this sort of analysis of the conceptual spheres of culture not only because of its intrinsic value, but also to gain a better understanding of the relations between the conceptual sphere and the social-cultural and ecological-subsistence spheres. This has been the purpose of this chapter; I hope that other researchers will be able to shed additional light on the basic issues raised here.

Appendix: The Story of the Woman and the Tapir

There was once a woman in the woods. Her husband left her in the woodland. So she met up with some bush pigeons who talked with her. The woman asked the pigeons to help her get out of the woods. She even fixed food for them but the food was too heavy and the pigeons didn't eat very much of it. The pigeons told the woman that they could not help her because they were too small and she was too big to carry while flying. The pigeons told the woman that she must get the monkeys who were coming up behind her to carry her out. The monkeys carried her slowly and with difficulty to a hammock in the woods after eating all the woman's food. The hammock was that of a tapir. The tapir returned (according to some informants he was away at this time) and asked the woman what she was doing there. The woman explained how the monkeys had carried her there and that she wanted to get home. "I couldn't get all the way home because they said I was too heavy and so they left me here in your hammock."

The tapir said that she could stay with him and get everything to eat. "You don't need nothing, I can look for food for you." The tapir took her as his woman. He was a male tapir. The tapir searched his neighbor's plantations for food. He didn't work at all. He look for corn, sugar cane, and cassava. He brought her food and she would eat. They stayed there for a while and she bore the tapir a baby, a little boy, the son of the tapir and the woman. The little boy grew up and stayed right there with his mama and papa. He, the father, stayed right there until the son was big.

One day, as he was leaving, the tapir told the woman, "Today I am going to look for something to eat for you. Maybe they will catch me in the place where I am stealing and they will kill me. If you see a little rain pass over that is because I am dead." The woman said all right, and that day the tapir went out and searched for food. It happened that day that a little rain passed and the woman said to her son, "Your papa is dead now." Some time before, the tapir had told the woman, "Any day you see I am dead, you must cut the ball skin and dry it. With that skin the boy will live. He'll get everything to eat and drink if you dry the skin of my balls."

The woman had two brothers, and the man who killed the tapir was the woman's elder brother. The brothers came to the woman and asked her what she was doing there. So the woman said, "I am waiting here because my man went out and never did come." The brothers told her he was stealing and they had shot and killed him because he was caught stealing cassava, sugar cane, and corn. She told them that they must cut off the balls because she wanted them for her boy to live on. The brothers agreed and cut off the balls and gave them to the mother who dried them in the hot sun.[6]

Now the boy turned into a good big man. His father was dead, so her brothers invited the woman and her son to come to their place to live. She and the boy went to live with her brothers. One day the brothers made fun of the boy's loud walk and said that he was not human but a tapir. So the boy ran away into the bush and turned into a tapir. He ran away because his uncle told him he was a tapir because he made too much noise with his feet.

Acknowledgments

Research was supported by grants from the National Institute of Mental Health, the Wenner-Gren Foundation, the Public Health Service, and the Duke University Graduate School. The research was carried out during the summer of 1969 and February through October of 1970. I would like to express my appreciation to my wife, Christine, for helping with the research and to Bernard and Judi Nietschmann, who rendered assistance on the first trip.

Notes

1. Eighty-nine percent of the five hundred Rama live on Rama Cay.
2. Other references to the manatee in early historical accounts include Roberts 1965: 97–98; Squier 1965: 130–137; and Bell 1899: 38–39.
3. It is interesting to note that the Rama may have used tapir femurs for making flutes (Conzemius 1927).
4. There are many other important points which should be made regarding these myths. The Rama tapir myth takes up the problem of inheritance in an oblique way by suggesting that the tapir lost his inheritance (i.e., fishing magic) to man and became the heavy-footed creature we know today. Likewise, in the Miskito version the tapir loses a cultural instrument of music (the flute) because he is heavy-footed and cannot climb a tree. The howler monkey, like man, knows when rain is coming, as did the tapir before he became the animal we know today. However, the howler monkey stands halfway between man and the tapir because he has attributes of both. Noise, habitat, weight, and culture are important concepts in analyzing the symbolism of these animals in the myths. In addition, the sexuality of the domestic crops (associated with women) is opposed to the potent male sexuality of the tapir in the Rama text.
5. There is some evidence to support the idea that historically both the manatee and the tapir were important in the cultures of the east coast of lower Central America. Olga Linares (personal communication) indicates that one small settlement of villages at Bocas del Toro, Panama, in 900 A.D. had a diet composed in good part of manatee, which accounted for about 25 percent of the butchered weight total (all animals included). No tapir bones were found in thousands of specimens, a fact which may mean that tapirs were overhunted at this time. Once the area was vacated, the tapirs came back, as did the other forest fauna. William Williams (1969: 232) mentions that tapirs were gone before 1740 in the south Rama area. Apparently they

returned later, in the nineteenth century, when we hear about them from Roberts, Squier, and Bell.

Nietschmann (personal communication) has asserted that older Miskito refuse to eat tapir and manatee meat. It is only recently, he says, that Miskito have begun to eat manatee and tapir meat in areas of Creole contact. He has also claimed (1973: 112) that tapirs and manatees were once "undesirable food animals." This may be questioned on the basis of the combined weight of the cosmological and archaeological evidence. His suggestion that "This dietary change may have come about as a response to the decline of other meat sources" (1973: 112) fits in with the hypothesis that environmental modifications by man produce changes in the distribution and numbers of flora and fauna which in turn affect the dietary preferences of cultures. Certainly, tapirs and manatees would be subject to cyclic changes in population size. The issue is whether these changes would affect the cosmologies of the lower Central American peoples. The evidence presented in this chapter suggests that the tapir and manatee have always been important symbolically in the lives of lower Central American peoples and in their cultures, in spite of the fact that these large mammals were not always available in abundance as a food source. Likewise, jaguars are *basic* to much of the lowland Middle and South American cosmology and myth, but not at all important as a direct food resource. For additional references to the symbolism of the tapir among South American Indians, see Lévi-Strauss (1969; 1973) and Wilbert (1970); on the symbolism of the manatee see Wilbert (1970).

6. Today, the Rama use the skin of the tapir's testicles to bring luck in fishing.

References

Bell, C. Napier, 1899. *Tangweera*. London: Edward Arnold.

Berckenhagen, H., 1894. *Grammar of the Miskito Language*. Bluefields, Nicaragua.

Conzemius, Eduard, 1927. Die Rama-Indianer von Nicaragua. *Zeitschrift für Ethnologie*, 59: 291–362.

———, 1932. *Ethnographical Survey of the Miskito and Sumu Indians of Honduras and Nicaragua*. Bureau of American Ethnology, Bulletin No. 106. Washington, D.C.: Government Printing Office.

Dampier, William, 1968. *A New Voyage Round the World*. New York: Dover.

Esquemeling, John, 1967. *The Buccaneers of America*. New York: Dover.

Furst, Peter T., 1968. The Olmec were-jaguar motif in the light of ethnographic reality. In Elizabeth P. Benson, ed., *Dumbarton Oaks Conference on the Olmec, October 28th and 29th, 1967*. Washington, D.C.: Dumbarton Oaks Research Library and Collection.

Hamilton, Kenneth G., n.d. Miskito myths and beliefs. Unpublished manuscript.

Kramer, Fritz, 1970. *The Literature of the Cuna Indians*. Ethnologiska Studier, No. 30. Göteborg, Sweden.

Lathrap, Donald W., 1973. Gifts of the cayman: some thoughts on the subsistence basis of Chavín. In Donald W. Lathrap and Jody Douglas, eds., *Variation in Anthropology*. Urbana: Illinois Archaeological Survey.

Lehmann, Walter, 1920. *Zentral-Amerika: Die Sprachen Zentral-Amerikas*. Teil. 1, Band 1. Berlin: Dietrick Reiner, Ernst Vohson.

Lévi-Strauss, Claude, 1963. *Totemism*. Boston: Beacon Press.

———, 1969. *The Raw and the Cooked*. New York: Harper and Row.

———, 1973. *From Honey to Ashes*. New York: Harper and Row.

Loveland, Franklin O., 1971. Salty dogs, or how I discovered the principle of life among the Rama Indians of eastern Nicaragua. Paper presented at the 70th annual meeting of the American Anthropological Association, New York.

Nietschmann, Bernard, 1973. *Between Land and Water*. New York: Seminar Press.

Ortner, Sherry, 1970. Food for thought. Unpublished Ph.D. dissertation, University of Chicago.

———, 1973. On key symbols. *American Anthropologist*, 75: 1338–1346.

Roberts, Orlando, 1965. *Narrative of Voyages and Explorations on the East Coast and in the Interior of Central America*. Gainesville: University of Florida Press.

Squier, E. G. (Samuel Bard), 1965. *Waikna: Or Adventure on the Miskito Shore*. Gainesville: University of Florida Press.

Wilbert, Johannes, 1970. *Folk Literature of the Warao Indians*. Los Angeles: Latin American Center, UCLA.

Williams, William, 1969. *Mr. Penrose: The Journal of Penrose, Seaman*, ed. David H. Dickason. Bloomington: Indiana University Press.

Part Two

BLACK POPULATIONS
AND THE ANGLO FRONTIER

Black Carib (Garífuna) Habitats
in Central America

WILLIAM V. DAVIDSON

As a result of Spain's failure to conquer and colonize the eastern Caribbean lowlands of Central America, this hinterland attracted English-speaking traders, woodcutters, and planters during the seventeenth and eighteenth centuries. The frontier also served as a place of refuge for Negro slaves and freemen seeking to escape Spanish society and West Indian plantations. Miscegenation between native peoples of northeastern Nicaragua and these African and Anglo newcomers produced a biologically mixed people with a predominantly Indian culture and language known today as the Miskito Indians.

On the island of Saint Vincent in the Lesser Antilles a similar biologically mixed but culturally Indian population had evolved by the early eighteenth century from escaped Negro slaves who sought refuge among the native Carib Indians. Because of their militant reaction to conquest these so-called Black Caribs were eventually deported from Saint Vincent by the British and resettled on the Bay Islands near Honduras in 1797. From here they gradually expanded along the mainland coast of eastern Central America until today Black Carib communities dot the shore line from Stann Creek, Belize, to Plaplaya in far northeast Honduras. In like fashion the Miskito have spread from their original location near Cape Gracias a Dios to include territory from Caratasca Lagoon in Honduras (close to the end of Black Carib settlement at Plaplaya) to Pearl Lagoon in southeast Nicaragua.

In spite of similar origins the Miskito are usually viewed today as Indians (although the term Zambo, referring to an Indian-Negro admixture, was often applied by Spanish speakers during the colonial period), while the Black Caribs are frequently considered an Afro-American population. A number of factors are responsible for this contrasting identification, not the least of which is the possibly greater degree of African admixture in the Black Carib population and the greater retention of African elements in Black Carib folklore, religion, and music (Solien 1959). Nonetheless, Black Caribs and Miskito have evolved comparable, though not identical, social structural adjustments to the particular demands of the frontier economy with which they interact (Helms n.d.).

Although both groups have maintained subsistence production during the nineteenth and twentieth centuries, Black Carib and Miskito men have sought opportunities for work at the coastal port towns or with various European and North American companies exploiting local resources. As was noted in the Introduction, the Miskito generally have adapted to the frequent absence of husband-fathers from villages and families via matrilocal residence. The Black Caribs have made a comparable adjustment by means of so-called consanguineal or matrifocal *household structures in which a series of liaisons or common-law partnerships link men and women for longer or shorter periods of time; male heads-of-household are frequently brothers and/or sons rather than legal husbands. In both cases groups of consanguineally related women provide the stabilizing core and central influence of the household and the family and also tend agricultural subsistence plots. Consequently, lengthy or irregular absences from home by men do not disrupt the social fabric.*

The Black Caribs are featured in the following essay in which William Davidson, a cultural geographer, details the distribution of their settlements with particular emphasis on different levels of "habitat."

Along the Caribbean coast of Central America minority cultures have persisted for several centuries in a Spanish-American political realm. Isolated from the higher, interior isthmus by physical geography and separate transportation systems, the Caribbean coastal peoples have created diverse patterns in their land and livelihood that greatly contrast with those of the majority Ladino culture. Today, the minority populations hold a fascination for social scientists primarily because they are little-known anachronisms of a pre-European heritage, they provide excellent material for cross-cultural studies of man-land relationships in a relatively homogeneous physical setting, and they are being assimilated at varying rates by a variety of agents.

One such group that has persisted as a recognizable, close-knit minority is the Black Caribs (Garífuna or *morenos*), who constitute the primary population inhabiting the shorelands of the Bay of Honduras (Figure 1). The Black Caribs first lived on Saint Vincent Island in the far southeast Caribbean, where the Afro-Amerindian population had its beginnings as a mixture of African slave and Island Carib Indian. But at the close of the eighteenth century the Black Caribs were

Figure 1   Distribution of Black Carib (Garífuna) Settlements in Central America, 1974

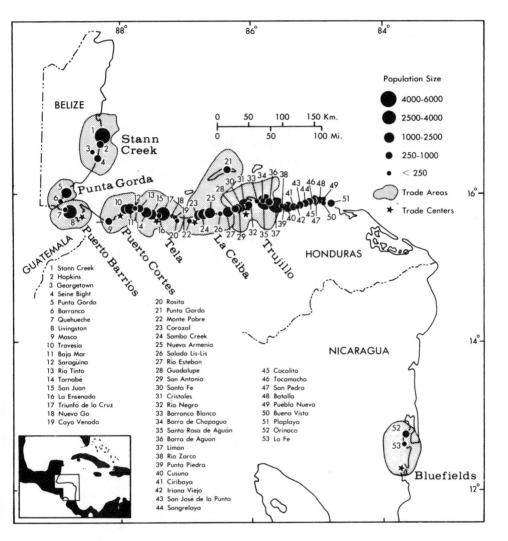

deported by the British Navy to the Bay Islands off the coast of Honduras. Subsequently they dispersed along the Caribbean coasts of Belize, Guatemala, and Honduras. Today the Negroid group still maintains its unity, primarily because the Black Caribs speak a common language known as Garífuna—the word they use to denote their culture.

The Black Caribs have been the subjects of several highly specialized and highly localized research projects, conducted almost entirely by anthropologists. The most prominent scholars of the Garífuna have been Douglas Taylor (1948, 1951a, 1951b) in linguistics, Nancie Solien González (1961, 1965, 1969) in household structure, and Pierre Beaucage (1965, 1966, 1970) in ethnohistory and economic anthropology. There have also been major contributions by Coelho (1955, 1964), Firschein (1961), Hadel (1972), Munroe (1964), and Sanford (1971). However, in these and other more general or earlier studies the extent of the modern Garífuna realm and facts about habitat have not been specifically noted.

This chapter constitutes the results of an initial portion of a study on the cultural geography of the Black Caribs. Under the co-sponsorship of the National Geographic Society and the research committee of my university, I conducted field surveys during the summer of 1973 to determine the range of the Black Carib habitat. Although my primary concern was to delimit the larger culture region, or *macro*-habitat, of the Black Caribs, this chapter also reports tentative identifications of Carib territory at other levels. Specifically, descriptions will follow for the gross distribution of settlements, the major physical settings of Black Carib villages (viewed here as *micro*-habitats), and their economic trade areas (*meso*-habitats).

Distribution of Settlements (Macro-Habitat)

Beginning at Stann Creek, Belize, and continuing south and east along the shore of the western Caribbean Sea until Plaplaya, Honduras, almost every coastal village is inhabited predominantly by the Garífuna people (Figure 1). Using aerial photographs and *in situ* censuses, I calculated that there are 77,000 (plus or minus 2000) Garífuna within this 400-mile stretch of coastline. They reside in settlements that average about 1500 inhabitants each (Figure 2). Six of the fifty-one settlements are in Belize, two are in Guatemala, and forty-three are under the political jurisdiction of the Republic of

Figure 2   Populations of Garífuna Settlements, 1974

```
Population

5000-5500   +
4000-4500   +
3500-4000   +
3000-3500   ++
2500-3000   ++
2000-2500   ++++
1500-2000   ++++
1000-1500   ++++
 500-1000   ++++++++++++ (12)
below 500   ++++++++++++++++++++++ (22)
```

Number of Settlements

Honduras (see Table 1). In addition, an isolated two-village enclave has been reported by Conzemius (1932: 7) and Nietschmann (1973) at Pearl Lagoon, Nicaragua. Only one village, founded when the Black Caribs were first stranded on Roatán Island, is not on the mainland.

The Garífuna are obviously beach folk. With only four exceptions, their settlements are located on beaches, less than two hundred yards from the sea. The "interior" settlements range as far inland as five miles. In Belize the single interior Carib village, Georgetown, is the result of a government resettlement project after hurricanes dam-

Table 1   Garífuna Population: Totals and Percentages by Country, 1974

Country	Approximate Garífuna Population	Garífuna Population as Percentage of Total for Country
Belize	10,600	8.0%
Guatemala	5500	0.11%
Honduras	60,900	2.5%
Nicaragua	800	0.04%
Total	77,800	

Sources: Field observations, 1970 Census of British Honduras, and Ruddle and Hamour 1972.

aged coastal Garífuna villages. (A second interior resettlement community, Silk Grass, no longer exists.) In Honduras Cayo Venado, Rosita, and Monte Pobre have grown near fruit company railroads to take advantage of a market for their fruits and oil-palm produce. One settlement eight miles inland from Limón was reported previously to be a Carib site (Helbig 1965: Map VI) but was found last July to be inhabited solely by Spanish speakers.

Generally Black Carib settlements are distributed in a highly agglomerated pattern. However, in Belize villages are separated by as much as fifty miles. The settlements of Honduras are much closer together, being on the average about five miles apart. This is the case particularly in extreme eastern Honduras, where thirteen villages are concentrated along a forty-mile stretch of coast. Villages normally have a linear pattern parallel to the sea that makes for small distances between them. In fact, a number of settlements are so near to each other and interact so frequently that they could be considered "twin villages" (Travesía-Baja Mar, Tornabé-San Juan, Cayo Venado-Rosita, Guadalupe-San Antonio, Cristales-Río Negro, Santa Rosa de Aguán-Barra de Aguán, Punta Piedra-Cusuna, Sangrelaya-Cocalito, Tocomacho-San Pedro, and Batalla-Pueblo Nuevo).

Less than 3 percent of the total number of Garífuna live outside the villages. Isolated single-family habitations are rare. There are, however, increasing seasonal migrations from the villages to the larger cities. Garífuna from northeast Honduras, for example, now work for up to four months at a time in interior towns such as Tegucigalpa, San Pedro Sula, and Santa Rosa de Copan, and there are increasing indications that Carib enclaves will develop in the larger cities. Also, a few thousand Garífuna reportedly live in New York, Boston, Los Angeles, and New Orleans, where they serve in the United States merchant fleet.

Sites of Settlement (Micro-Habitats)

The sites chosen by the Garífuna for permanent settlement can be grouped into four major categories according to features found in the local environments. The most consistent feature, of course, is beachland. Except for the four "artificial" settlements established by government agencies or founded in response to fruit company business, each Black Carib settlement is located on the sea. As Douglas Taylor, a prominent student of the Garífuna, has put it: "To the Carib it is unthinkable that he should settle permanently in any place not immediately accessible to the sea" (1951a: 62).

In addition to the littoral setting, the beach folk apparently prefer that at least one of the following natural features be present: a small stream, a river mouth or estuary, a protected bay, or a lagoon to the interior. Figure 3 illustrates in idealized diagrams the four predominant micro-habitats of the Black Caribs. In these local settings the Garífuna practice their fishing and agriculture, generally at a level of subsistence. The river mouth–beach combination accounts for about 40 percent of the settings.

Trade Areas (Meso-Habitats)

Although most economic activities of the Black Caribs are carried out within the immediate vicinity of their settlements, in recent times trade contacts with distant towns have occurred on a regular basis. In fact, most Garífuna villages are now attached to a larger, usually non-Carib population center in a trade network. Eight such trade centers (shown in large type on Figure 1) and their hinterlands can be identified. Within the trade areas there is at least weekly contact between each village and the trade center. Only in eastern Honduras between Punta Piedra and Plaplaya are the settlements so isolated that frequent trade contacts do not occur with the larger coastal towns.

It is yet unknown whether such concentrations of Black Carib settlement as those around Puerto Cortes, Tela, La Ceiba, and Trujillo are the results of non-Carib urban growth, or whether the urbanization occurred because the centers were placed near areas of dense Garífuna habitation. At any rate, today the trade centers are primary sources of the cash income and the innovations that are being introduced into Black Carib villages. It is within the framework of these economic "meso-habitats" that the Garífuna are being drawn into the mainstream of Central American life.

It would seem of some value to organize future discussions of culture and habitat to include various levels of territory, as I have done here. The concept of habitat can relate both to the nature of the physical environment and to its spatial quality. "Habitat" might prove to be more useful if thought of not only at the level of the culture region but also at lower levels, such as those of the "micro-habitats" and "meso-habitats" analyzed in this chapter. In the search for several

Figure 3 Diagrams of Typical Garífuna Settlement Sites

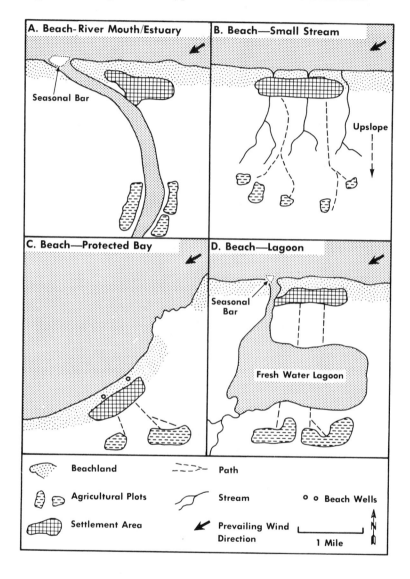

A. Beach-River Mouth/Estuary

Seasonal Bar

B. Beach—Small Stream

Upslope

C. Beach—Protected Bay

D. Beach—Lagoon

Seasonal Bar

Fresh Water Lagoon

Beachland

Agricultural Plots

Settlement Area

Path

Stream

Prevailing Wind Direction

o o Beach Wells

N

1 Mile

habitat boundaries within the all-encompassing culture region, the researcher will find that the fundamental unity of the larger region—which normally first attracted our attention—no longer over-shadows the subregions. The smaller regions may be no less impor-tant. In the study presented here the habitats of economic subregions and local settings were found to be quite significant in the affairs of the Black Caribs themselves.

References

Beaucage, Pierre, 1965. *Ethno-histoire et changement sociale chez les Caraibes Noirs du Honduras.* Maitries Sciences Sociales, Department de Sociologie et d'Anthropologie, Université Laval, Quebec, Canada.

———, 1966. Les Caraibes Noirs: trois siècles de changement social. *Anthropologica,* n.s., 8: 175–195.

———, 1970. Economic anthropology of the Black Carib of Honduras. Ph.D. dissertation, University of London.

Coelho, Ruy Galvao de Andrade, 1955. The Black Carib of Honduras: a study in acculturation. Ph.D. dissertation, Northwestern University.

———, 1964. Os Karaib Negros de Honduras. *Revista do Museo Paulista* (São Paulo), 15: 4–212.

Conzemius, Eduard, 1932. *Ethnographical Survey of the Miskito and Sumu Indians of Honduras and Nicaragua.* Bureau of American Ethnology Bulletin No. 106. Washington, D.C.: Government Printing Office.

Firschein, I. Lester, 1961. Population dynamics of the sickle-cell trait in the Black Caribs of British Honduras, Central America. *Americal Journal of Human Genetics,* 13 (2): 233–254.

González, Nancie L. Solien, 1961. Family organization in five types of migratory wage labor. *American Anthropologist,* 63: 1264–1280.

———, 1965. The consanguineal household and matrifocality. *American Anthropologist,* 67: 1541–1549.

———, 1969. *Black Carib Household Structure: A Study of Migration and Modernization.* American Ethnological Society Monograph No. 48. Seattle: University of Washington Press.

Hadel, Richard E., S.J., 1972. Carib folk songs and Carib culture. Ph.D. dissertation, University of Texas, Austin.

Helbig, Karl M., 1965. *Areas y paisajes del nordeste de Honduras.* Tegucigalpa: Banco Central de Honduras.

Helms, Mary W., n.d. Domestic organization in eastern Central America: the Cuna, Miskito, and Black Carib compared. Unpublished manuscript.

Munroe, Robert L., 1964. Couvade practices of the Black Carib: a psychological study. Ph.D. dissertation, Harvard University.

Nietschmann, Bernard Q., 1973. *Between Land and Water: The Subsistence Ecology of the Miskito Indians, Eastern Nicaragua.* New York: Seminar Press.

Ruddle, Kenneth, and Mukhtar Hamour, eds., 1972. *Statistical Abstract of Latin America, 1970.* Los Angeles: Latin American Center, University of California.

Sanford, Margaret S., 1971. Disruption of the mother-child relationship in conjunction with matrifocality: a study of child-keeping among the Carib and Creole of British Honduras. Ph.D. dissertation, Catholic University of America, Washington, D.C.

Solien, Nancie L., 1959. West Indian characteristics of the Black Carib. *Southwestern Journal of Anthropology*, 15: 300–307.

Taylor, Douglas M., 1948. Loan-words in Central American Carib. *Word*, 4: 187–195.

————, 1951a. *The Black Carib of British Honduras*. Viking Fund Publications in Anthropology, No. 17. New York: Wenner-Gren Foundation.

————, 1951b. Sex gender in Central American Carib. *International Journal of American Linguistics*, 17: 102–104.

Carib-Creole Relations in a Belizean Community

SHEILA COSMINSKY

The most tangible and lasting evidence of British interests in eastern Central America is the now self-governing colony of Belize, formerly British Honduras, which anticipates full independence in the not-too-distant future. The origins of the fledgling nation can be traced to the buccaneers of the Spanish Main, who found the isolated east coast of Yucatán an excellent location for rest and rendezvous. A permanent settlement was established near the mouth of the Belize River by the end of the seventeenth century, when British woodcutters began to exploit rich stands of logwood which produced a valuable dye much sought after in Europe. When logwood ventures began to decline after the mid-eighteenth century British lumbermen turned to mahogany, which for a century or so was in great demand by shipbuilders, makers of fine furniture, and manufacturers of railroad coaches.

Belize City also became a financial and import center for much of Central America. British and North American goods in particular were traded to Guatemala and Yucatán, with Belize merchant-bankers handling the financial transactions involved. Imported European and North American goods received in exchange for exported forest products also sustained the colony itself, for local agriculture was largely ignored in favor of the more lucrative lumbering. When forestry began to decline in the late nineteenth century, local subsistence agriculture was forced to expand, but agricultural growth and diversification remain major problems for the future nation (Ashcraft 1973).

Although a small country, Belize is characterized by an unusual degree of cultural and linguistic diversity. Black Caribs, "Creoles," Spanish-speaking mestizos, and Mayan Indians form the major population components, and East Indians, Europeans, Chinese, and Lebanese are also found. Creoles, who account for at least half of the national population, are descendants of the early

95

European lumbermen ("Baymen") and the African slaves and freemen who labored in the forests. Black Carib populations began to enter the country after 1800. Many Mayan Indians and Spanish-speaking mestizos came to British Honduras in the late nineteenth century in the aftermath of an uprising of Indians and mestizos in Yucatán known as the War of the Castes. Other Maya arrived from Guatemala at various times.

Not surprisingly, these diverse population components have created a complicated web of interethnic relations. In the following essay Sheila Cosminsky examines a number of areas of interethnic conflict or cooperation in the town of Punta Gorda, a district capital situated on the coast of southern Belize. Her analysis focuses particularly on relationships between Creoles, who though fewer in number hold the most important economic and political positions, and the Black Caribs, who definitely are the majority population in Punta Gorda but usually have been restricted to positions of little, if any, power and influence.

This chapter describes and analyzes the relationships between two ethnic groups, Black Caribs and Creoles, in Punta Gorda, a coastal town in southern Belize. I will focus on the following problems: first, the criteria of ethnic differentiation utilized by the members of the different groups; second, the extent to which these stereotypes correspond with "objective" differences, or rather, with my observations; third, the relationships between these groups; and fourth, the degree to which ethnicity is a determinant of behavior and social relations.

Two levels of analysis are employed. One level concerns the shared or distinctive institutions and traits of the groups. The other concerns the patterns of social interaction, seen in a behavioral frame of reference. This dual analysis is based on the assumption that in populations characterized by wide cultural variability the analysis of social differentiation must proceed together with the study of cultural differentiation. As Michael G. Smith stresses (1965: 55), without this coordination of cultural and sociological study, acculturation is deprived of its social reference and stratification is inadequately conceived in terms of race, caste, or class. Barth has recently emphasized that the maintenance of ethnic boundaries by groups in contact implies "not only criteria and signals for identification, but also a structuring of interaction which allows the persistence of cultural differences" (1969: 16). The rules allowing and preventing interaction in different social situations will be analyzed and the implications of the ethnic stereotypes for group relations will be discussed.

Methods and Historical Background

My data were gathered mainly during the summer of 1965 in Punta Gorda, the somewhat isolated administrative center of the Toledo District of Belize.[1] A combination of participant observation and informant questioning was employed. Instead of imposing categories, I used people's own terms for the relevant groups in formulating questions. I noted both the respondents' remarks and the context in which they were made. Other questions were of a social-distance type, regarding friendship, marriage, and other relations. Answers to questions about hypothetical situations were contrasted with actual observations.

According to the 1960 census, the de jure population of the town was 1789 persons. The census reports do not include any breakdown of ethnic groups. However, using a sample of 1574 names from the Malaria Health Survey, together with a combination of information from officials, personal knowledge, and the criteria of surname, an approximation can be made: 69.6 percent of the town population was Black Carib and 17.5 percent Creole; the remainder was composed of a few Spanish (5.1 percent), East Indians (5.7 percent), Chinese (1.1 percent), and others (1.0 percent).

The Black Caribs are descendants of escaped Negro slaves and "Red" or Island Carib Indians who inhabited Saint Vincent Island and Dominica. In 1797, after an uprising against the English, they were deported to the Bay Islands, from where they fled or dispersed to the mainland coast of Honduras, Guatemala, and Belize. (This arrival is celebrated and reenacted annually by the Caribs on Carib Settlement Day, November 19; the celebration plays a role in reinforcing Carib identity and unity.) Caribs were settling in British Honduras by 1802. For the most part the Caribs stayed by themselves, fished, and went to their farms, often located far up the Moho, Temash, or Río Grande rivers. Increasing numbers of men became wage laborers in mahogany camps and sugar plantations.

In 1868, after the United States Civil War, immigrants from the southern states settled in Toledo District and established sugar plantations, nutmeg plantations, and mahogany camps. Today there are only two large sugar estates and rum breweries left in the area. To many of the inhabitants this represents a decline in the economic condition of the district. East Indians were brought in as indentured laborers, many of them to work on these estates. Today most of the East Indians are independent rice farmers who live outside of town.

Creoles and Spanish also moved into the area to work in the camps and plantations.

The term "Creole" refers to descendants of Africans, with or without European admixture, who speak English or Creole (a dialect of English spoken widely throughout the West Indies). Some informants specified that a Creole was anyone born in the country with Negro ancestry other than Carib. As the town grew, merchants, civil servants, and government officials moved in. These were usually Creoles or Englishmen, some of whom intermarried with Creoles. Mayan Indians live in the inland villages several miles outside of Punta Gorda; they come to town for marketing, for hospital services, and on official business.

Although Black Caribs are numerically in the majority in Punta Gorda, the town is controlled politically and commercially by non-Caribs. The subordinate position of the Caribs and dominance of the Creoles should be viewed in national and historical perspective. Though Creoles are numerically fewer in Punta Gorda they are *nationally* the predominant group, composing about 60 percent of the total population of Belize. The Creole center was around Belize City, the former capital; therefore they were trained by the British for various civil servant positions and became administrative officers throughout the country. The Creoles were also better off economically and thus had more capital for commercial enterprises than the Caribs. These historical conditions have reinforced and may even have contributed to the ethnic stereotypes. González (1969) feels that economic competition, among other factors, contributed to the present-day situation in which the Black Caribs are set apart as being "different" from and "inferior" to other black groups in the area. Within the town there is a coincidence of two stratification systems, ethnic and economic, which will be discussed later.

Group Images and Stereotypes

What images or stereotypes do Creoles have of Caribs and vice versa?[2] Table 1 shows the Carib responses to differentiating criteria. The Creole image agrees with the Carib conceptions concerning language, occupation, house type, diet, dress, and religion. Creoles stress physical criteria more than the Caribs, mentioning that Caribs have "big heads" and "big feet," the former attributed to their mixed ancestry and the latter to their going barefoot. They also mention that Carib

Table 1 Carib Conceptions of Group Differences

Criterion	Carib	Creole
Language	Carib	Creole, English
Occupation	Fisherman, farmer	Merchant, civil servant
House	Thatched roof	Corrugated iron roof
Diet	Plantain, fish, cassava	Rice, beans
Dress	Careless, no shoes	Better, more expensive; shoes
Religion	Catholic	Anglican, Methodist
Physical features	Darker skin	Lighter skin
Character, attitudes	Sincere, steady, hospitable, friendly, work hard, loud, clannish	Insincere, feel and act superior, work hard, proud, vain

women carry provisions and baskets on their heads, whereas Creole women do not. The main difference lies in the Creoles' conception of character traits. They share the Carib view that Creoles are ambitious and hard-working. But while the Creoles regard Caribs too as ambitious and eager for knowledge, they also consider them rough, loud and expressive, superstitious, thieving, and boastful. Creoles say further that Caribs are clannish, that Carib men are lazy although the women work hard, and that Caribs smell.

Observed Differences

The differences presented as part of the folk images will now be discussed in relation to observed differences. How do the stereotypes coincide with "reality," if at all? Differences that were not mentioned in the stereotypes, but which were observed, will also be discussed.

Language is the most important criterion of differentiation, being mentioned either first or second by every informant. The Carib language derives from that of the Island Caribs with the addition of French, Spanish, and West African influences and loan words (Taylor 1951). Among the Carib people, Carib is spoken in the home as the primary language and in most public and private conversations. Eighty-nine percent of the Caribs also speak English (1960 census), and field work was conducted primarily in English.

The Carib language is a crucial aspect of Carib identity and history. Caribs will scold their children for speaking Creole, which they regard as "bad" or "broken" English. Language is also used by some non-Caribs as a reason for not associating with or for disliking Caribs.

A few Creole informants said they did not know when they were being talked about because they could not understand Carib. Other Creoles said they would like to learn Carib, but that it is too difficult (though they usually had not tried).

Many Caribs also speak Spanish, especially those who were born in or have relatives in Guatemala. In addition, many Caribs can speak Creole and several can speak one or both of the Mayan Indian languages (Mopan and Kekchi) spoken in the nearby Indian villages. This multilingualism and ability for languages is one of the few Carib characteristics that are praised by the Creoles and others. It is regarded as something inherent in the Caribs, as a native ability or racial trait. The high degree of multilingualism may be related to, and reinforced by, the social and psychological rewards it provides for the Caribs, since it is one means by which they can feel superior to others.

Children of interethnic marriages usually speak the language of the mother. If the mother is Carib the child speaks Carib, while if the father is Carib the child may not learn that language. This may be one way in which it is possible for a mixed child to "pass" or to become more accepted by the Creoles.[3]

Creoles speak Creole, which is usually their primary language, and English. The census category of English, however, also includes Creole, which is not officially considered a separate language. A few Creoles may speak Spanish as their primary language because they were born in Guatemala or because they were of mixed ancestry and their mothers were Spanish. Since East Indians, Chinese, Syrians, North Americans, Britishers, and others also speak English there is not a one-to-one correlation between language and ethnicity among the Creoles. However, since only Caribs speak Carib as their mother tongue, there is a perfect correlation in this case.

Regarding occupation and economic activity, both Caribs and Creoles hold the stereotype that Carib males are fishermen and females work the land, while the Creole tends to be in a governmental position or commerical job. Some Creoles, as I pointed out earlier, remarked that the Carib man is lazy and the woman works hard.

In actuality, there are few fishermen today; perhaps six to ten dories (dugout canoes) put out on an average day, although more go out on Wednesday and Saturday, the market days. Out of 224 Carib males on the voters list (*British Honduras Gazette,* 1964), nineteen gave their occupation as fisherman and fourteen listed themselves as farmer or planter. (Of the 125 Creole males on the list, six listed as fisherman and twelve as farmer.) Most Carib fishermen fish part-time. Very few are full-time, large-scale fishermen. Those who do fish work in the early morning hours and are free the rest of the day. This different working pattern may have contributed to the Creole image of the Carib male as lazy. The number of Caribs fishing fluctuates with the availability of wage labor and other jobs. Since the amount of money earned by small-scale, part-time fishing is relatively little, this type of fishing is more of a subsistence activity than a money-making one. On weekdays the amount earned may vary from seventy-five cents to two Belizean dollars and on market days from three to eight dollars. Despite the small number of fishermen, both Caribs and Creoles perpetuate the image of the Carib as a fisherman.

Most Carib agriculture is performed in the Saint Vincent Block, often called the "Carib Reserve," an area of 960 acres just behind the town. Any Carib not of alien parentage born in Punta Gorda, or anyone married to or living with a Punta Gorda-born Carib, has a share in the land. Each head of family pays a tax of fifty cents annually which goes toward the total tax to be paid to the government. Only a small proportion of the Carib households have applied for land and Creoles criticize that because much of the land is not being used. Males clear the land while women do most of the tending and harvesting, but not all women farm. Rice is the primary crop, both for consumption and for market, with cassava a secondary crop. Pineapples, plantains, beans, and other crops are also grown.

Some Caribs are carpenters or tailors or are engaged in other service occupations. Most are wage laborers, often working at seasonal jobs and therefore frequently unemployed. Forty-eight percent of the Carib male voters listed themselves as laborers, while only 20 percent of the Creoles did. Most Carib men have migrated at some time to other parts of the country as mahogany loggers, citrus workers, laborers for the United Fruit Company, or seamen on steamers and freighters; or they have gone to the United States for various jobs. Several Carib women have worked as domestic servants for non-Carib families in Guatemala or Belize City. Wage-labor jobs have shifted with the pattern of the economy.

Teaching is one area of employment that has long been open to Caribs; they have provided the bulk of the teachers, especially for rural villages, partly because few others are willing to live under the conditions found in many rural areas. Religious affiliation is another factor, since schools are denominational and most of the schools in the Indian villages have been established by the Catholic Church. Because the Caribs are Catholic, they are employed as teachers in these schools. However, Caribs are rarely appointed to high positions in the schools in the larger towns or in Belize City. These positions are usually filled by priests, nuns, American Papal Volunteers, and Creoles.[4] Previously many higher-status positions and civil servant jobs were closed to Caribs, who for this reason went into teaching. However, the prestige of teaching has declined, particularly because of the relatively low pay and poor living conditions, and many Carib teachers have resigned.

Civil servant and clerical positions are occupied mainly by Creoles and East Indians; only recently have a few Caribs obtained such positions.[5] The storekeepers and club or canteen owners are mainly non-Carib, too. Of nineteen merchants in Punta Gorda nine were Creole, three were Spanish, three were Chinese, two were Carib, one was Syrian, and one was Mayan. One of the few Caribs who does own a small store used to work for one of the English store owners, and when the owner died he went into business for himself.

Most agricultural produce, meat, and large fish are sold in the marketplace by Carib and Spanish vendors, some from other Carib villages and from Guatemala. People are tending to buy more items such as plantains and rice rather than cultivate them. The few Creoles who engage in agriculture have larger farms, some ninety acres or more, outside of town, and hire laborers to work the land, in contrast to the subsistence-scale cultivation of the Caribs. The patterns of land tenure are thus different for the two groups; the Caribs hold a block of land in common and the Creoles independently own large shares of land.

To sum up the matter of occupation, the largest difference between Caribs and Creoles is the virtual nonexistence of Caribs in commercial jobs, except as petty traders. In other categories, especially the broad one of laborers, there is overlap of the ethnic groups. Thus the occupational stereotypes held by the people themselves do not coincide precisely with the actual situation; however, the relative proportions of the ethnic groups in various occupations do tend in the direction indicated by the stereotypes.

House types range from those with thatched roofs, wooden frames, and earthen floors to those with corrugated iron roofs, raised wooden frames, and wooden floors. Creole informants and many Caribs said that Caribs live in thatched-roof houses and Creoles in ones with iron[6] roofs, but now the pattern is starting to change. Only about 49 percent of the approximately 225 Carib houses are thatched. I did not see any Creoles living in thatched houses; however, one can find them in such accommodations in other parts of the country. In most of the town, thatched houses are scattered and members of different ethnic groups are also dispersed, often living next door to each other. Economics is a prime consideration, since thatch is cheaper than iron. Another factor is prestige and status. Civil servants, merchants, policemen, and others of high status almost always have a raised house with an iron roof. More and more teachers are also building this type of dwelling. When someone moves up the social scale he moves into a house of this kind, regardless of ethnicity.[7]

Although many of the older people and more "traditional" Caribs live in thatched houses, which have become a symbol of "Caribness," particularly in the eyes of the Creole, the stereotype does not hold in actuality. There is just a grain of truth in it. The predominant tendency is for Creoles not to live in thatched houses, whereas Caribs live in all types.

The main food of the Caribs is a stew of pounded plantain, fish, and coconut milk called *hudut*. Fried fish and plantain are also often eaten. Cassava is important, mainly in the form of cassava bread. According to Conzemius (1928), the main staple food of the Carib was cassava bread. Today, however, this is secondary to plantains and rice, and is made less frequently than before.

Rice and beans are the staples of the Creoles. Although Caribs also eat rice, none of my Creole informants eat either *hudut* or cassava bread. Creoles also eat fish, though less often than the Caribs, and beef, pork, and chicken when available. Creoles seem to eat more vegetables than Caribs and to buy more canned food. Although much of the diet is similar among the different ethnic groups, the staple foods are different and agree with the stereotypes.[8]

With respect to religion, the Catholic church, established there about 100 years ago and now run by an American priest, is the largest in Punta Gorda. According to the 1960 census, 86 percent of Punta Gorda residents are Catholic. Almost all the Caribs and Spanish in town are Catholic. The few Creoles who are members either seem to be of mixed Creole-Spanish ancestry or are from Guatemala. The Methodist church is the second-largest, being composed mainly of Creoles and East Indians (6 percent of the residents). The Anglican church, which is smaller (5 percent of the residents), is composed of Creoles. The Jehovah's Witnesses and the Nazarene church are recent additions and are growing. Their membership includes all ethnic groups.

Although they are Catholic, many Caribs also maintain elements of their "traditional" beliefs. These beliefs, which are not shared with other ethnic groups, focus on dreams, spirits, the honoring of ancestors, certain ceremonies such as the *dogo,* and the Carib religious specialist, the *buiai.* Although not all Caribs hold the beliefs or have attended a *dogo* ceremony, they all know of such matters, and the "traditional" religious elements serve as symbols of Carib identity for many Caribs.[9]

These observations show a correlation between the stereotype of religious affiliation and actual church ties. Caribs are Catholic and Creoles are primarily Anglicans and Methodists. The few who do not fit this pattern are usually of mixed parentage or are dissatisfied with the church. The church thus tends to increase the social distance between Caribs and Creoles.

Most informants mentioned that physical differences exist between the different ethnic groups. When asked to specify differences, however, they had difficulty in doing so. Several Caribs and Creoles said that the Creole had fairer skin color. A few, however, pointed out that many Creoles were as dark as some Caribs. The Creole emphasizes that he is the "son of the Baymen," and the Carib tends to emphasize his Carib Indian (which one informant said was a "white race") rather than his African ancestry.

To the outsider, physical features are not very reliable differentiating criteria between Carib and Creole. "Creole" includes any person of black ancestry, other than a Carib, with or without European admixture, and covers a wide variety of shades of skin color from very dark to very fair. In Punta Gorda the majority of Creoles are lighter than the majority of Caribs. However, there is a wide area of overlap of skin color.

Most of the people in town dress in similar fashion. The differences are primarily among the older women. Some older Carib women wear longer, loose skirts and headscarfs, particularly when working around the house or going out to the fields. Some go barefoot, too, while Creoles do not. However, many of these women are beginning to wear cheap plastic sandals.

Although only a couple of informants mentioned surname as a differentiating criterion, I found it quite useful. The surnames of most Caribs are Hispanic, such as Martinez, Lopez, Avila, or Enriquez, or else are purported to be traditionally Carib, such as Arzu and Parchu. A few Caribs have English-derived names, such as Daniels and Nicholas, but these are usually different from the local Creole names. Creoles usually have English names such as Johnson,

Foster, and Vernon. (In cases of mixed offspring the surname might be misleading. A child with a Carib mother and a Creole father will have a Creole name but will be identified as a Carib.) Although there are a few cases of overlapping names and a few cases of intermarriage, names do provide a clue to the ethnic identity of the majority of people in Punta Gorda.

Zones of Interaction and Noninteraction

Studies of interethnic and interracial relations have shown that whenever different groups come into contact certain patterns of avoidance and social distance develop which reduce the possibilities of conflict. To be sure, most spheres of social relations have aspects of both interaction and noninteraction, but usually one will predominate over the other. I will use a situational frame of reference to analyze the relationships in Punta Gorda, adapting Gluckman's concepts of social situation and crosscutting allegiances (1958). The situations that will be analyzed relate to marriage, friendship, visiting, dances, child loaning, religion, education, politics, and economics.

Endogamy is the stated ideal for all ethnic groups. The Caribs' and Creoles' most frequent objections to intermarriage with each other are that one should not "mix blood" and that the Carib way of life is too different and too hard. Endogamy is the general practice as well as the ideal, and is supported by strong family pressures. Carr and Thorpe's statement (1961) that intermarriage is common in Punta Gorda is not borne out by the data. I was aware of only nine intermarriages. In every case either one or both of the mates had come from outside Punta Gorda. Therefore those who deviate from the norm usually marry someone from outside the town. In contrast, of the six unmarried mixed couples of whom I knew, both parties either had been born in Punta Gorda or had lived there for some time.

Informants said that in cases of intermarriage a Carib boy will marry a Creole or Spanish girl, that is, will marry up, but rarely will a Creole boy marry a Carib girl. This generalization is supported by the limited data available. In the nine intermarried couples, a group which contained other ethnic groups besides Caribs and Creoles, five of the males were Carib. Only one of the females was classed as Carib, and she was actually one-half East Indian and one-half Carib. On the other hand, in the six unmarried couples only one of the males but four of the females were Carib. The ethnic breakdown of these couples is shown in Table 2.

Attitudes toward offspring of interethnic matings seem to be largely an individual matter. One man whose father is Carib and whose mother is mixed Creole and East Indian said he feels more accepted by Creoles. This may be because of his style of living and his position as a civil servant. In general, if one parent is Carib the child is regarded as Carib, while if one parent is Creole and the other non-Carib (for example, Spanish or East Indian) the child is regarded as Creole. However, how an individual identifies himself is a more complex matter. Whether a Spanish-Creole identifies with one group or the other depends on the situation and to whom he is reacting or talking.

There are few interethnic relationships of friendship and visiting. Some East Indians and Creoles are friends, but Carib-Creole friendships and house visits are rare. When asked to describe their friendship preferences, people said they preferred friends from their own group. When asked about preferences outside of their own group, both Caribs and Creoles said they preferred Spanish friends. The most frequent reason was that they are "steady, sincere, and

Table 2 Interethnic Couples

Number	Male	Female
	Married	
1	Carib	Creole ($\frac{1}{2}$ Creole, $\frac{1}{2}$ Mayan)
1	Carib	Creole
2	Carib	Spanish
1	Carib	Carib ($\frac{1}{2}$ East Indian, $\frac{1}{2}$ Carib)
1	Spanish	East Indian
1	Creole	East Indian
1	East Indian	Creole
1	Chinese	Creole
	Unmarried	
1	Carib	Creole
3	Creole	Carib
1	East Indian	Carib
1	Mayan	Creole

make good friends." "You always know how you stand when dealing with the Spanish. When they are for you, they are for you, and when they are against you, they are against you." The Caribs contrast these qualities to those of the Creoles, who, they feel, are insincere; they cite examples of how a Creole will act as a friend of a Carib in some circumstances in Punta Gorda, but in other circumstances, such as a meeting in Belize City, will act as if he does not know the Carib.

Public dances are held every weekend during the summer. Both Carib and Creole males attend them. Carib girls go to these dances, but Creole or Spanish girls do so only rarely unless it is a special occasion. One Creole girl said that her father would not allow her to go. Carib girls dance with males from any ethnic group, while the few Creole girls who attend will not. Creole boys attend most of the dances and usually will dance with anyone.

The caretaker system is characteristic of Black Caribs (Solien 1959, González 1969). A young child is sent to live with another family, usually of a higher economic and social position. His services are exchanged for food, shelter, and education. These cases may cut across ethnic lines. Although in one case a three-year-old Creole child was being raised by a Carib family, more frequently a Carib child is loaned to a Creole or English family in the capital or in Stann Creek in order to obtain an education. Sometimes the Catholic Church acts as caretaker. At least three Carib male informants had been raised for several years by a Catholic priest at the Catholic Mission. One Creole informant had been brought up by the Anglican minister in Monkey River because his family was very poor. Although these informants expressed their appreciation for the opportunities and education they had received, they were also highly critical and resentful of certain restrictions and discrimination they felt they had experienced during such relationships.

As mentioned earlier, most Caribs are Catholic and most Creoles are Methodist or Anglican. These religious differences reinforce the prevalent noninteraction between Caribs and Creoles. Since the church plays an important role in socialization, it supports ethnic noninteraction from an early age. A close relationship exists, moreover, between education and religion. The primary schools are denominational, although government-supported. One primary school is Catholic and the other is Methodist. Most of the students in the Catholic school are Caribs (although some are Spanish), the teachers are nuns, and the assistant teachers are Caribs. The Methodist school has Creole and East Indian students and teachers. The few Caribs

who attend the Methodist institution are either dissatisfied with the
nuns or the priest, have not done well in the Catholic school, or are of
mixed parentage. The principal of the Methodist school said he had
made it clear to the students that he would not stand for any acts of
open prejudice. The fact that he felt it necessary to say this implies
there is potential conflict.

In 1960 a secondary school, St. Peter's Claver College, opened in
Punta Gorda. There students prepare for the examinations for the
General Certificate of Education from Cambridge University. The
enrollment in 1965 was 72 persons, with 16 students graduating. The
teachers are mainly Papal Volunteers from the United States. Previously, if a student wanted a secondary education, he had to go to
Belize City or to Stann Creek. Most could not afford this, although
sometimes the child was given to a family which he would serve in
return for his educational expenses. This practice drained top students from the local area. The new school is increasing the educational opportunities for many who could not afford to go to high
schools in other towns. Many of the graduates will become teachers,
especially in the rural Mayan villages.

In general, the primary educational institutions, like their associated religions, reinforce noninteraction patterns between Caribs
and Creoles. The secondary school is more mixed and offers increased opportunities, especially for the Caribs, who place a high
value on education. Although the bulk of primary school teachers in
the country are Caribs, more Creoles have been able to gain higher
education and obtain higher-level jobs. This situation may now be
starting to change as more Caribs obtain a higher education and better opportunities.

Politics is an increasingly important sphere of joint participation
and interethnic contact. There are two political parties in town: the
People's United Party (PUP), which is the party in power, and the
United Democratic Party (UDP), the opposition party. (The latter was
known until 1975 as the National Independence Party.) The PUP in
Punta Gorda is composed mainly of Caribs, although a few Creoles
and others who possess political and economic power also belong.
Most Creoles and Spanish in town tend to support the UDP, as do a
good number of Caribs. Therefore, although the PUP is almost entirely Carib, the political parties cut across ethnic lines in that some
members of all ethnic groups belong to the UDP. Politics is a dominant area of interest and conversation, and many activities such as
dances, meetings of social clubs, and the like are organized along

party lines. Ethnic relations are influenced by these activities. There are also subtle manipulative relations involved in the interplay of ethnicity and politics, by means of which certain Creoles obtain and maintain power over Caribs.

The mayor of the town is a young Creole and PUP member. He is also the son of a senator, an appointive position filled by the governor. Most of the political and economic power in the town is concentrated in his family. The representative in the Legislative Assembly is a Carib from Punta Gorda, also a PUP member, but elected by a very narrow margin. The local governing body is the Town Board, made up of seven members elected for three years. All are PUP members and the majority are Caribs. The primary administrative and judicial authority in Punta Gorda is the district officer. The district officer during my stay was a Creole who expressed many of the stereotypical opinions about Caribs. The other civil servants and clerks are from various ethnic groups. One path for economic and political advancement for Caribs is the civil service; by this means some Caribs have broken through some of the barriers of discrimination. However, since civil service positions were usually located in Belize City and now are in Belmopan, the new capital, and in other parts of the country, these Caribs must leave Punta Gorda, draining the town of its local talent.

On the whole, in Punta Gorda ethnicity seems to be decreasing as a basis for political groups. In many situations political affiliations and interests link ethnic segments and, at least on the surface, override ethnic allegiances.

Economic transactions in stores and the marketplace are also areas for ethnic interaction. These contacts involve complementary, but relatively impersonal and secondary, relationships. On market days Carib women congregate at the marketplace to sell and buy agricultural produce, meat, and fish. Hardly any Creoles come to the market. Those who have Carib domestics send them to do the marketing, and other items they buy in the stores. Men mix more than women, particularly in the drinking at the taverns and clubs.

It should be apparent by now that economic structure tends to coincide with ethnic stratification. There are basically two classes in Punta Gorda: an upper class of merchants and government officials, who are non-Carib, and a lower class which is made up of the rest of the population. Within the upper class there are ties of marriage, kinship, and friendship. (There is virtually no middle class, although there is much variation within the two established classes. The teachers form a separate clique and one might view them as an incipient middle class.) The few Caribs who are either storeowners or officials are not considered part of the upper class or elite.

Since the majority of the upper class is generally of lighter skin color, the color-class system, as proposed by Raymond Smith (1956), seems at first glance to be appropriate. According to Smith, in British Guiana and most of the British West Indies social stratification is based on a hierarchical ranking of color and occupation. The latter keeps the system open and mobile to a limited degree, so that there is not a one-to-one correlation between color and status. However, the emphasis lies on the value placed by all groups on color differences. In Punta Gorda, in contrast, the factor of ethnicity overrides that of color. There are some Creole storeowners, businessmen, and others in the local upper class with very dark skin. On the other hand, there are no Caribs in this group regardless of skin color.

Another feature of the status system that Smith considers important is that ethnic groups which do not fit readily into the color-class hierarchy, such as the Chinese and East Indians, are able to infiltrate at all levels and to take over functions for which a relative lack of status consciousness is an advantage, particularly in the retail and distributive trades. Although there are a few Chinese in these trades in Punta Gorda, the majority are Creoles who generally are very status-conscious.

There are relatively few opportunities for wage labor in town or in the district for any ethnic group. Those who want jobs or advancement, or are discontented with the economic conditions in the area, migrate either temporarily or permanently. So Caribs start off in the teaching profession and then move into some branch of the civil service, while others work at a variety of wage-labor jobs. As a Carib advances he adopts a lifestyle comparable to that of a Creole of similar occupation and class, including appropriate status symbols such as a raised house with an iron roof, a kerosene or gas stove, a latrine or bathroom, and a water vat.

I suggest that the lack of economic competition in town, together with the migration of the ambitious and discontented, is an important factor in the relatively low degree of conflict observed, at least overtly, between ethnic groups. There are tensions and prejudices as manifested in the stereotypes, remarks, and social-distance patterns of the majority of townspeople. However, the atmosphere is not one of hostility but rather of "live and let live." In areas where there is greater economic competition between Caribs and Creoles, such as in Stann Creek and Belize City, there also seems to be a higher degree of interethnic conflict.

Summary and Conclusions

Multiple criteria are used in differentiating ethnic groups, and they vary with the context and individual informant. Not everyone believes or accepts the stereotypes completely. Some informants accept certain criteria but not others (for instance, language but not physical features). Certain Creoles said Caribs were ambitious; some said they were lazy; others said both. This may not really be a contradiction. The informant may have at least two different models and be relating to different interaction experiences he has had or has heard about. Still other cases he may regard as individual exceptions.

Those situations in which members of different ethnic groups jointly participate usually involve secondary relationships characterized by one or more of the following conditions:

1. Two or more representatives of the groups are mutually dependent. Examples would include commercial transactions and economic participation.
2. One person needs the other and profits from the relationship, while the other suffers no loss. Such situations would include relations of adoption, *obeah* and curing, dances, and godparenthood.
3. External forces or laws compel all groups to participate. These relations would include those that are nationally influenced, such as in education and certain political situations.
4. The interaction is unavoidable, incidental, or of short duration. These contacts include meetings of various associations and encounters on the streets and inside public buildings.

However, in the realm of primary relationships, such as marriage, friendship, and visiting, noninteraction and avoidance patterns are the rule. Family, school, and church reinforce the social distance between Creoles and Caribs. These are also the institutions in which children participate; thus they are socialized to the existing ethnic images and relational patterns. (See Brockmann 1973 for a discussion of similar patterns among Spanish and Creoles in northern Belize and Mazzarelli n.d. for Spanish-Creole relations in western Belize.)

Social distance both supports and is supported by the stereotyped conceptions of the ethnic groups and the auxiliary symbols of cultural differences such as names, songs and dances, and language. Moreover, close and frequent contacts do not necessarily change stereotyped conceptions. As Berelson and Steiner point out, "personal contact with members of ethnic minorities does not automatically increase or reduce tensions; it can do either or neither" (1964: 510). Informants who most clearly and openly expressed opinions and described incidents concerning ethnic relations were those who had more extensive contact with members of other groups through various jobs and travels. These informants were between twenty and forty years of age. In contrast, the older Caribs, particularly the women and even those who had worked elsewhere with other groups, tended to make general comments such as "everyone gets along here; each person minds his own business" and "Caribs used to not mess around with anyone, but now everyone mixes." All informants, except for one Creole, said that relations between the groups are better now than previously even if the local economic conditions may not be so.

Those people who are ambitious leave Punta Gorda to find jobs elsewhere. As more Caribs gain economic opportunities there will be an increasing amount of intragroup stratification. Within Belize as a whole social class may be becoming a more important determinant of social interaction than ethnicity, or at least may be providing alternative ties. But on the local level in Punta Gorda, where social mobility necessitates leaving town, there is still little class stratification within the Carib segment, and ethnicity is a more predominant determinant of group affiliation than is economic position. Within the Creole segment, however, there are distinctions between the upper and lower class, and principles of class stratification probably structure social relations to a larger degree than among the Caribs.

The lack of economic competition and opportunities is causing dissatisfaction among many people. The non-Carib storeowners and officials stay, while those who want to move upward migrate. This pattern tends to maintain the relationship between the ethnic and class stratification systems on the local level and also keeps down competition and conflict.

Some of the discontented channel their activities into politics. The two political parties contending for power, and their internal schisms, provide a set of relations that cut across ethnic loyalties. In certain situations political alliances are stronger to some people than those based on ethnicity. While ethnic identification is still an extremely important factor in social relations, politics is becoming an increasingly important focus of activity and is providing alternative ties.

Whatever the situation, there is an element of choice open to the individual concerning the way he defines the social situation and which ties he will manipulate. To understand what is happening, one must investigate how the various allegiances of ethnicity, class, and politics are interwoven and how the individual evaluates each one.

Notes

1. The field work was conducted under the auspices of the Brandeis University Summer Field School Program. A return visit in January 1975 confirmed the trends noted earlier.
2. Information on ethnic relations with Spanish, East Indians, and Indians is included in an unpublished field report, "Interethnic Relations in Punta Gorda, British Honduras: A Preliminary Report," Brandeis University, 1966.
3. I suggest for future investigation the hypothesis that a mixed offspring with a Carib father would "pass" more easily or face less discrimination by non-Caribs than one with a Carib mother.
4. This tendency may be gradually changing; one Carib is now the head of the Teachers Training School in Belize City.
5. Although the East Indians living outside of town are rice farmers, those in town are mainly civil servants, clerks, or laborers.
6. The people actually refer to this material as zinc.
7. Some people who say they are too poor for such a house are probably referring not only to their economic ability to construct it, but also to the expense of purchasing concomitant symbols of status such as a stove, furniture, and water vat.
8. The sharpest differences in material culture arise from those items that are involved in food preparation, including graters, sieves, and the *wola* or *ruguma* (woven cassava drainer), all used in preparing cassava, and the mortar and pestle used to thresh rice.
9. The Caribs distinguish their beliefs from notions of illnesses, accidents, and deaths caused by *obeah*, "de Laurence magic," or what one Carib called "voodoo tricks," in which many also believe. These latter practices are widespread among Creoles and some Spanish and East Indians, although they have been declared illegal.

References

Ashcraft, Norman, 1973. *Colonialism and Underdevelopment: Processes of Political Economic Change in British Honduras.* New York: Teachers College Press.
Barth, Fredrik, 1969. *Ethnic Groups and Boundaries.* Boston: Little, Brown.
Berelson, Bernard, and Gary A. Steiner, 1964. *Human Behavior.* New York: Harcourt, Brace and World.
British Honduras Gazette, Supplement. List of Voters for the Toledo South Electoral Division for 1965. December 19, 1964. Belize City.

Brockmann, C. Thomas, 1973. Mestizos and Creoles in northern Belize. Paper presented at the meeting of the Society for Applied Anthropology in Tucson, Arizona, April 12, 1973.

Burdon, Major Sir John Alder, 1934. *Archives of British Honduras,* Vol. II. London: Sifton Praed.

Carr, David, and John Thorpe, 1961. *From Cam to Cays.* London: Putnam.

Census of British Honduras. 1960. Belize City.

Conzemius, Eduard, 1928. Ethnographic notes on the Black Carib. *American Anthropologist,* 30: 183–205.

Gluckman, Max, 1958. *An Analysis of a Social Situation in Modern Zululand.* Rhodes-Livingston Papers, No. 28. Manchester: University of Manchester Press.

González, Nancie L. Solien, 1969. *Black Carib Household Structure: A Study of Migration and Modernization.* American Ethnological Society Monograph No. 48. Seattle: University of Washington Press.

Mazzarelli, Marcella, n.d. Ethnicity and power in a multi-ethnic community in British Honduras. Unpublished manuscript.

Smith, Michael G., 1965. *The Plural Society in the British West Indies.* Berkeley: University of California Press.

Smith, Raymond, 1956. *The Negro Family in British Guiana.* London: Routledge and Kegan Paul.

Solien, Nancie L., 1959. West Indian characteristics of the Black Carib. *Southwestern Journal of Anthropology,* 15: 300–307.

Taylor, Douglas M., 1951. *The Black Carib of British Honduras.* Viking Fund Publications in Anthropology, No. 17. New York: Wenner-Gren Foundation.

Tumin, Melvin, 1952. *Caste in a Peasant Society.* Princeton: Princeton University Press.

Part Three

NATIVE ADAPTATIONS TO AN ECONOMIC HINTERLAND

Dietary Diversity and Nutritional Security in a Coastal Miskito Indian Village, Eastern Nicaragua

DOROTHY J. CATTLE

In the following essay Dorothy Cattle presents a detailed analysis of the annual dietary diversity of the villagers of Little Sandy Bay, a Miskito community on the coast of eastern Nicaragua. Since 1968–1969 the residents of Little Sandy Bay, along with other coastal Miskito, have been involved in commercial hunting of green sea turtles for sale to foreign companies which supply gourmet restaurants in Europe and North America. With the income from this work the villagers purchase a number of foodstuffs from local stores, augmenting their diet of subsistence crops, fish, and game.

Cattle finds that the villagers' annual intake of protein, fats, and carbohydrates varies significantly depending on how much cash is available to purchase "store food" and on the locally produced subsistence food available. Her conclusions indicate that greater reliance on store food provides greater dietary diversity, but that contrary to "common-sense" expectations, periods of greatest food diversity during the year are also periods of below-average nutrient intake! Furthermore, the sea turtles which provide cash when sold are also an important subsistence food. Therefore Cattle concludes that cash has upset the equilibrium presumed to exist between the indigenous subsistence pattern and the nutritional adaptation of the villagers. Large disruptions may be in store for the Miskito, at least from a nutritional and subsistence point of view.

In some ways the turtle boom represents simply the latest in a series of short-lived commercial activities in which foreign companies have briefly exploited a local resource and provided foreign material goods and foods to the Miskito in return for labor or other services. Indeed, boom-and-bust economic conditions have been a factor of Miskito life for close to 300 years. Since the late seventeenth century, when the arrival of European buccaneers

117

initiated the first boom, the Miskito have collected tortoise shell, sarsaparilla, skins, and India rubber for trade with European trading agents; they have served as laborers for foreign mahogany contractors, tapped rubber, worked in gold and silver mines opened in the mountainous interior, grown bananas for the Standard Fruit Company, and labored for pine-lumbering firms (Helms 1971). The historical documents and ethnographic data indicate that in the periods between "booms," when foreign companies left the region and store supplies dwindled, an increase took place in local subsistence activities. These had not been entirely abandoned at any time, since agriculture, an important source of food, is largely women's work. The subsistence economy (including agricultural products, fish, and game) then supported the population until the next foreign speculators arrived.

The new predicament faced by contemporary Miskito turtle fishermen lies in the heavy commercial exploitation of a traditional subsistence item. If the coastal Miskito are unable to find a suitable alternative for the turtle meat which they utilized before the arrival of the foreign commercial turtle companies, local subsistence may not be sufficient to support the coastal population during "bust" conditions (cf. Nietschmann 1973: 238–244). As Cattle indicates, however, the Miskito local subsistence base is diversified, and includes in addition to turtle a number of agricultural products, pigs and chickens, game, and river and ocean fish. Therefore, contrary to the predictions of total systemic collapse dramatically put forth by some investigators (Nietschmann 1974), it can be predicted that when turtling declines the coastal Miskito will once again increase their subsistence agricultural efforts in addition to continuing their hunting and fishing; they may also explore the possibilities of greater reliance on animal husbandry (currently practiced by riverine Miskito more than by coastal groups).

A related and perhaps greater problem portending subsistence and nutritional dislocations lies in the continuing growth of the Miskito population. This is not just a recent phenomenon. The fact that the Miskito have increased greatly during the last three centuries, growing from considerably less than one thousand persons at the time of European contact to 40,000 or more today (Helms 1971: Chapter 1), would seem to evidence successful adaptation to the boom-and-bust conditions to date. But if population increase finally reaches the point where indigenous subsistence production can no longer support the populace between foreign economic booms, greater hardships, including nutritional difficulties, may be expected and new forms of adaptation will have to emerge.

On the national or international level, numerous studies (Insull et al. 1968; Bedford 1946; Areskog et al. 1969; Gopalan and Raghavan

1969; ICNND 1960) have been conducted to assess the nutritional problems of particular countries or large sections of the population, covering such matters as the urban-rural dichotomy and different income groups. Community nutritional surveys are also relatively abundant (Flores et al. 1964; Jyothi et al. 1963; Scrimshaw et al. 1953). The focus of both types of surveys is often very specialized, ranging from problems of economics (Périssé et al. 1969; McKigney 1968) and the green revolution (Borlaug 1972) to malnutrition (Gopalan 1967; Jelliffe 1963) and energetics (Ramanamurthy and Dakshayani 1962; Bradfield 1971). Many nutritional studies call for social, cultural, and environmental information. Anthropologists form a growing minority of contributors to nutritional studies of non-Western groups. Leonard Joy states one aspect of nutritional studies: "we are concerned with the level and nature of [food] consumption and its pattern between people and over time" (Joy 1973: 202). Others (Berg et al. 1973; György and Kline 1970) recognize the need for quantitative data and systematic methods of looking at aspects of nutrition. These methods are most developed in the clinical assessment of nutrition and health problems. Economics is also making an increasingly important contribution to the study of productivity and nutritional status. What are lacking are systematic and quantitative contributions from anthropology. This study represents an initial contribution in this area. Based on a village food consumption survey conducted in a Miskito Indian village, it examines a dietary diversity measure using quantitative data.

Ethnographic fieldwork was carried out from February 1972 through March 1973[1] on the east coast of Nicaragua. The study village is Little Sandy Bay, an isolated Miskito Indian community of 377 persons located 75 miles north of the nearest port town of Bluefields. Marine, coastal, and inland resource zones are exploited by the village. Local ecosystem foodstuffs are obtained from turtling,[2] swidden agriculture, animal husbandry, hunting, fishing, and gathering. Green sea turtle (*Chelonia mydas*) has always been an abundant and dependable subsistence resource for the coastal Miskito, although the picture is rapidly changing. The resource is now sold commercially by the coastal Miskito to a foreign-owned company. This arrangement provides the only source of cash income for Little Sandy Bay. Purchased food items[3] are obtained from two major village stores and several minor ones which are operated by villagers. Store inventories include food staples such as rice, sugar, flour, coffee, and beans and nonfood items such as cloth, cigarettes, notebooks, and soap. There are no health services in the village.

The Problem and Methodology

The purpose of this study is to examine the diversity of the annual dietary pattern of the Little Sandy Bay Miskito group from the perspective of protein, fat, and carbohydrate intake.[4] There are at least twelve variables or complexes of factors which could have nutritional consequences for the Miskito. These are: (1) household size; (2) household composition; (3) subsistence procurement equipment per household; (4) village demography; (5) amount of available land; (6) amount of land devoted to swidden agriculture; (7) health; (8) kinship networks; (9) seasonality and availability of local ecosystem foodstuffs; (10) income patterns; (11) dietary diversity; and (12) market-economic and local ecosystem risks. This chapter will explore the measurement of dietary diversity. It will be argued that such diversity indicates, in the case of the coastal Miskito, disequilibrium in their subsistence and nutritional adaptation to the local ecosystem.

The problem of diversity, stability, and security has been approached by economists, anthropologists, ecologists, and others (Adams 1968; Lee and DeVore 1968: 30–55, 78–84, 92, 99–110, 221–228). It is a matter of ongoing discussion in the various disciplines. It has been generally assumed that the greater the dietary diversity, especially of local ecosystem foods (that is, the larger the number of different food items exploited), the more secure the nutritional strategy. This, as we shall see, is not necessarily the case. Rather than viewing diversity as a static, reliable indicator of stability and security, I will suggest a broader view of the system of adaptation. "Security" is defined in this discussion as the maintenance of the average intake of nutrients. (For nutritional assessment "security" could be defined as the maintenance of recommended or required intakes of nutrients.)

No detailed information is usually available on annual food consumption patterns. Diets of non-Western groups are often characterized as based on one or two staples or are described as dependent on one major protein source and one or two carbohydrates. Non-quantified statements of the diversity of food available to particular groups probably distort the actual nutritional strategies employed. Such statements are too imprecise to serve as a basis for the assessment of nutritional strategies. The research reported here was intended as a step toward the necessary precision.

In Little Sandy Bay a preliminary inventory of the stores was made to determine what items were stocked and what quantities were on the shelves. All subsequent deliveries to stores were noted during interviews and checked with the bills of lading. Weekly interviews of the storekeepers were also conducted in order to record small, irregular purchases of beans, rice, and other items. Within the village records were kept of the number of turtles, game animals, and domesticated animals butchered. Weights were determined either by direct measurement, by the amount of meat sold, or by estimates made by the villager involved in the butchering. Estimates of agricultural yields for tuber crops were made from sample plots and by weighing the yield from several tuber plantings. The village census, conducted in January 1973 and recorded by household, provides information on the amount of land planted, the number of different cultigens, the subsistence procurement equipment owned (guns, turtle nets, boats, and the like), and the number of domesticated animals.

On the household level a food consumption survey was made. A 10 percent random sample of households was selected each seven days. Daily visits were made to each household during the week and a recall of foods consumed that day was recorded. A daily record was also kept of the number of food consumers per household in each of six age categories.

There are several factors that support the accuracy of this household food consumption survey. First, most foodstuffs enter the household in standard weighed or measured units. Weight units, pounds and half-pounds, are used for flour, rice, sugar, beans, and meat. Measured units include tablespoons and pints. Numerical units, such as five mangos or a "hand" (for bananas, cosco, and plantain), were used when recalling local fruits. Mean weights were determined for several local ecosystem foodstuffs, including breadfruit and tubers. A second reason to believe the survey was accurate is that interview questions were included to register minor items and to determine the size or quantity of unmeasured food items. Third, food preparation methods were observed, especially when unfamiliar items appeared in the survey, and specific recipes were collected.

In assessing the data it is first necessary to choose a measure of diversity and present it in such a way as to demonstrate its fluctuations or stability throughout the year. Next, dietary diversity must be related to the nutrient intake. Are low-diversity months correlated with a lower intake of one or more of the nutrients? If not, has compensation occurred by intensive exploitation of a local ecosystem food?

Such a measure of dietary diversity can be generally useful for comparisons of intercultural food consumption patterns. Comparative studies of dietary diversity, using a standard measure, may provide anthropologists with a range of variability for diversity. In other words, the measure may be fruitful for developing hypotheses about subsistence activities and diet, or cultural organization and diet. A standard measure of dietary diversity might be useful in diachronic studies as one way of determining the impact of change on a group. For instance, the impact of monoculture on the diet might be clearly shown in the reduction of dietary diversity, or the effect of newly introduced purchased food items might be reflected in either an increased or a decreased diversity. No one, to my knowledge, has examined the range of variability in dietary diversity.

Two measures of dietary diversity are presented here, followed by an explanation of why the second is more useful. Then the Miskito dietary diversity is analyzed in terms of its relationship to nutrient intake and security.

Measures of Dietary Diversity

The first measure of diversity in the diet is easy to conceptualize and to compute.[5] It is graphically presented in Table 1, which shows the number of food items that contribute to the Miskito nutrient intake per month. The table indicates an apparent lack of diversity in purchased foods but an apparent diversity in sources of nutrients from the local ecosystem.[6] The table also gives an idea of the seasonality of local ecosystem foods. However, it does not quantify the proportion contributed by each food item nor is there any information about the three nutrient categories. Much information is lost when using this measure, and since it does not measure distribution but only the number of items its usefulness for comparative purposes may be limited.

The second measure of dietary diversity, the Shannon-Wiener function (Krebs 1972: 506–507), combines two components of diversity, namely the number of items and their equitability—or the proportion contributed by each food item. A greater number of food items utilized per month, and a greater equality of their proportions in the diet, will increase the diversity index. The index is decreased when there is a greater contribution made by one food item in relation to the others or when the actual number of items is smaller. The index, H, is defined by the equation

$$H = -\sum_{i=1}^{S} (p_i)(\log_2 p_i),$$

where S is the number of food items and p_i is the proportion of the total sample belonging to the ith food item. The Shannon-Wiener function also enables one to compute H_{max}, the maximum dietary diversity of the monthly sample (that is, the diversity under conditions of maximum equitability):

$$H_{max} = -S(1/S)(\log_2 1/S) = \log_2 S,$$

where S again is the number of food items exploited by the group. One can then calculate the equitability, E, which ranges from zero to one:

$$E = H/H_{max}.$$

The food consumption survey provides the number of food items utilized by the Miskito Indians as well as proportions of the total contributed by each item in the three nutrient categories: proteins, fats, and carbohydrates. The monthly intake of these nutrients per consumer and the yearly average are also available.[7] Figure 1 presents the application of the Shannon-Wiener dietary diversity measure to the Miskito consumption data. Equitability ranges from zero to one. The position of the three nutrients in the middle range indicates immediately that not all resources are utilized equally and that not all resources contribute to the diet of the Miskito in any month. However, comparative studies may supply further information as to whether this Miskito position is extreme or normal.

If we examine the protein diversity line, which displays the most extreme changes of the three nutrient lines,[8] we notice a low point in June. The explanation involves other data from the food consumption survey. Commercial sales of turtle are banned by the Nicaraguan government from May 15 to July 15; this is a conservation policy to protect the gravid females as they migrate south to the Costa Rican nesting beach. The month of June falls in the middle of this ban on commercial sales of turtle. Cash income is depressed, limiting the amount of purchased food available to the villagers. In that month turtle is contributing over 70 percent of the dietary protein. Thus the protein diversity index goes down. This drop does *not* reflect any change in protein intake per consumer for the month of June. The steep rise in the protein diversity line for the month of July reflects either more equal contributions of protein by the various foodstuffs or an increase in the number of foods exploited. The food consumption data show that there were 12 foodstuffs contributing protein for the month of June and 23 for July, with less dominance by turtle in the latter month. However, in July protein intake per consumer

Table 1 Dietary Diversity (Nonquantified)

May	June	July	August	September	October
rice	rice	rice	rice	sweet bun	rice
sugar	sugar	sugar	sugar	rice	sugar
lard	flour	lard	lard	sugar	coffee
flour	coffee	flour	flour	flour	bread
coffee	bread	coffee	coffee	coffee	beans
bread	beans	bread	bread	bread	
beans	***	beans	beans	beans	***
	turtle	***	***	***	whelks
***	dasheen	eggs	eggs	turtle	turtle
turtle	cocoplum	turtle	whelks	supa	orange
shrimp	coconut	sea grape	turtle	shrimp	fish (sea)
plantain	cassava	plantain	plantain	plantain	deer
mango	cane (sugar)	mango	orange	orange	dasheen
fish (sea)	banana	krabu	hog	hog	cosco
fish (all)		hog	gibnut	fish (sea)	corn
dasheen		fish (river)	fish (river)	deer	coconut
corn		fish (sea)	fish (sea)	dasheen	cassava
cocoplum		fish (all)	fish (all)	cosco	breadfruit
coconut		dasheen	deer	corn	banana
cassava		cosco	dasheen	coconut	
cane (sugar)		corn	cosco	chicken	
beef		coconut	corn	cassava	
banana		cocoyam	coconut	breadfruit	
aji		cassava	chicken	banana	
		breadfruit	chicha		
		banana	cassava		
			breadfruit		
			beef		
			banana		
			aji		

Purchased food items appear above the asterisks, local ecosystem foods below them.

Table 1 (Continued)

November	December	January	February	March
sweet bun	sweet bun	sweet bun	sweet bun	sweet bun
rice	rice	rice	rice	rice
sugar	sugar	sugar	sugar	sugar
lard	lard	lard	lard	lard
flour	flour	flour	flour	flour
coffee	coffee	coffee	coffee	coffee
bread	bread	bread	bread	bread
beans	beans	beans		beans
			***	
***	***	***	turtle	***
eggs	eggs	turtle	plantain	yampi
turtle	turtle	hog	hog	turtle
plantain	shrimp	fish (river)	fish (river)	plantain
hog	hog	fish (sea)	fish (sea)	mango
gibnut	fish (sea)	deer	dasheen	hog
fish (river)	deer	dasheen	cosco	fish (river)
fish (sea)	dasheen	cosco	coconut	deer
deer	cosco	coconut	cassava	dasheen
dasheen	coconut	cocoyam	breadfruit	cosco
cosco	cocoyam	cassava	beef	coconut
coconut	chicken	breadfruit	aji	cassava
cocoyam	cassava	beef		breadfruit
chicken	breadfruit	banana		beef
cassava	beef	aji		banana
cane (sugar)				aji
banana				
armadillo				
aji				

Purchased food items appear above the asterisks, local ecosystem foods below them.

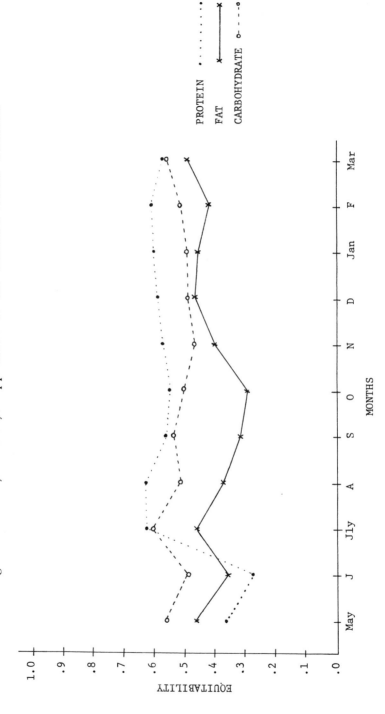

Figure 1 Dietary Diversity: Application of the Shannon-Wiener Function

Table 2   Nutritional Security and Dietary Diversity

Nutrient	Month	Intake Per Consumer	Yearly Average Intake Per Consumer	Diversity
Protein	June	47.7 g	47.16 g	low
	July	37.8 g	47.16 g	high
Fat	October	16.24 g	14.91 g	low
	May	5.43 g	14.91 g	high

dropped by 10 grams, to a yearly low of 37.8 grams (see Table 2). Here is one particular case in which dietary diversity does not equal security.

Utilizing the same perspective on the diversity line for fat, we find that the October low point is a reflection of the dominance of coconuts, which contribute somewhat over 76 percent of the fat for that month, although 15 other food items also contribute. This low point in the diversity index again is not reflected in a lowered dietary intake of fats; the intake is 1.33 grams above the yearly average. The relatively higher diversity for the month of May (20 items contributing fat and less dominance by coconuts) is concomitant with a below-average intake (nearly 10 grams per consumer below the yearly average). This is a second example contradicting the assumption that the higher the dietary diversity, the greater the nutritional security. A similar example could be presented for the month of July for the nutrient carbohydrate.

Conclusion

Further work needs to be done to assess the overall annual pattern and to test the significance of the observed fluctuations. However, these limited examples suggest that greater dietary diversity does not lead to greater nutritional security in all situations. Dietary diversity might be related to *compensatory* mechanisms of the nutritional strategy. In the particular situation of the Miskito, cash derived from the commercial exploitation of a basic subsistence resource—the green sea turtle—is seriously disrupting the subsistence and nutritional adaptation of the village. This in turn is disrupting the intensity and efficiency of food utilization. Cash income derived in this way is one factor that has upset the equilibrium of the adaptive system. The high dietary diversity displayed for particular months may be more a reflection of "food scrounging" than of efficient exploitation.

There appear to be two cases of high dietary diversity. One, which is in accord with general ecological principles, occurs when the adaptative system is in equilibrium, and the other occurs at a time of *disequilibrium*. The second kind may indicate the last peak before the occurrence of large disruptions which force a restructuring of the system along different lines (Krebs 1972: 545 et seq.). The Miskito are an instance of the second case. The standard measure of dietary diversity presented here represents one aspect of dietary disequilibrium. It brings out the disruptive interaction between the cash economy and the traditional subsistence system, and leads to the suspicion that the Miskito are in a very vulnerable position with regard to subsistence. High dietary diversity, in this particular example, appears to represent a critical point in the yearly round of a nutritional system which is already fragile.

Notes

1. I accompanied Brian E. Weiss, who was kind enough to share his grant and fellowship money with me.
2. The green sea turtles are captured by nets or harpoons.
3. "Purchased" food items are defined here as those which are outside the local ecosystem of the Miskito; "nonpurchased" foods are those that occur within the local ecosystem.
4. Excluded from the discussion are the other two major categories of nutrients—vitamins and minerals—as well as a consideration of foodstuffs as sources of energy (calories).
5. See Pielou 1969 for a discussion of quantitative measures of diversity.
6. A total of forty food items are utilized by the Miskito. Scientific names for selected food items are as follows: aji, *Donax* sp. (small surf clam); banana, *Musa cavendishii;* breadfruit, *Artocarpus communis;* sugar cane, *Saccharum officiarum;* cassava, *Manihot dulcis;* cocoplum, *Chrysobalanus icaco;* coconut, *Cocos nucifera;* cocoyam, *Xanthosoma* sp.; corn, *Zea mays;* cosco, *Musa* sp. (variety of banana); dasheen, *Colocasia esculenta;* gibnut, *Cuniculus paca* ssp.; krabu, *Byrsonima crassifolia* (nance); mango, *Mangifera indica;* orange, *Citrus sinensis;* plantain, *Musa paradisiaca;* sea grape, *Coccoloba uvifera;* supa, *Guilielma utilis* (pejibaye); whelks, *Tegula* sp. Yampi is a variety of yam. This information is derived from Nietschmann (1973: 247–253 and personal communication) and Brian E. Weiss (personal communication).
7. Brian E. Weiss, personal communication.

8. An appropriate test of significance has not yet been applied to the fluctuations discussed.

References

Adams, Robert McC., 1968. Early civilizations, subsistence, and environment. In Yehudi A. Cohen, ed., *Man in Adaptation: The Biosocial Background.* Chicago: Aldine.

Areskog, N. H., Ruth Selinus, and B. Vahlquist, 1969. Physical work capacity and nutritional status in Ethiopian male children and young adults. *American Journal of Clinical Nutrition,* 22 (4): 471–479.

Bedford, T., 1946. *The Health of the Industrial Worker in India.* Report of the Industrial Health Research Board of the Medical Research Council in the United Kingdom. Simla, India: Department of Health, Government of India.

Berg, Alan, Nevin S. Scrimshaw, and David L. Call, eds., 1973. *Nutrition, National Development, and Planning.* Proceedings of the International Conference on Nutrition, National Development, and Planning, held at the Massachusetts Institute of Technology on October 19–21, 1971. Cambridge, Mass.: M.I.T. Press.

Borlaug, Norman, 1972. Genetic improvement of crop foods. *Nutrition Today,* 7: 20–21, 24–25.

Bradfield, R. B., ed., 1971. Assessment of typical daily energy expenditure. *American Journal of Clinical Nutrition,* 24: 1403–1493.

Flores, M., B. Garcia, Z. Flores, and M. Y. Lara, 1964. Annual patterns of family and children's diet in three Guatemala Indian communities. *British Journal of Nutrition,* 18: 281–293.

Gopalan, C., 1967. Malnutrition in childhood in the tropics. *British Medical Journal,* 4: 603–607.

Gopalan, C., and K. V. Raghavan, 1969. *Nutrition Atlas of India.* Hyderabad, India: National Institute of Nutrition.

György, P., and O. L. Kline, eds., 1970. *Malnutrition Is a Problem of Ecology.* New York: S. Karger.

Helms, Mary W., 1971. *Asang: Adaptations to Culture Contact in a Miskito Community.* Gainesville: University of Florida Press.

ICNND (Interdepartmental Committee on Nutrition for National Defense), 1960. *Ecuador: Nutrition Survey.* Washington, D.C.: Government Printing Office.

Insull, William, Jr., T. Oiso, and K. Tsuchiya, 1968. Diet and nutritional status of Japanese. *American Journal of Clinical Nutrition,* 21: 753–777.

Jelliffe, D. B., 1963. The incidence of protein calorie malnutrition of early childhood. *American Journal of Public Health,* 53: 905–912.

Joy, Leonard, 1973. Nutrition intervention programs: identification and selection. In A. Berg et al., eds., *Nutrition, National Development, and Planning.* Cambridge, Mass.: M.I.T. Press.

Jyothi, K. K., et al., 1963. A study of the socio-economic, diet and nutritional status of a rural community near Hyderabad. *Tropical and Geographical Medicine,* 15: 403–410.

Krebs, Charles J., 1972. *Ecology.* New York: Harper and Row.

Lee, Richard B., and Irwen DeVore, eds., 1968. *Man the Hunter.* Chicago: Aldine.

McKigney, J. I., 1968. Economic aspects of infant feeding practices in the West Indies. *Journal of Tropical Pediatrics,* 14: 55–59.

Nietschmann, Bernard, 1973. *Between Land and Water.* New York: Seminar Press.

———, 1974. When the turtle collapses, the world ends. *Natural History,* 83: 34–43.

Périssé, J., F. Sizaret, and P. Francois, 1969. The effect of income on the structure of the diet. *FAO Nutrition Newsletter,* 7: 1–5.

Pielou, E. C., 1969. *An Introduction to Mathematical Ecology.* New York: Wiley-Interscience.

Ramanamurthy, P. S. V., and R. Dakshayani, 1962. Energy intake and expenditure in stone cutters. *Indian Journal of Medical Research,* 50: 804–809.

Scrimshaw, N. S., et al., 1953. Health aspects of the Community Development Project, Rural Area, Turrialba, Costa Rica, 1948–1951. *American Journal of Tropical Medicine and Hygiene,* 2: 583–592.

Cuna Household Types and the Domestic Cycle

REGINA E. HOLLOMAN

The subject of matrilocal residence has been raised several times in the preceding pages, generally in the context of post-Conquest adaptations to frontier economic conditions. In the following selection Regina Holloman details the range of variation in household form and function among the matrilocal San Blas Cuna on the island of San Ignacio de Tupile in the San Blas archipelago off the Caribbean coast of eastern Panama. The norm of household organization among the Cuna involves a married couple living in a house owned by the wife; with them live their married daughters, sons-in-law, and grandchildren and any still unmarried sons. The men of the household, that is, father-in-law and sons-in-law, comprise the agricultural work team responsible for producing subsistence crops, while the women cooperate in kitchen and household duties. Holloman notes a number of variations from this norm, but finds that, in spite of a growing tendency for younger men to prefer neolocal residence, the matrilocal pattern still predominates.

Holloman attributes the continuity of matrilocality to three main factors. First, the amount of time involved in subsistence agriculture by the father-in-law and sons-in-law of the average household is sufficiently small so that each man has considerable time to devote to other activities—including village politics, cash cropping of coconuts (see the chapter by Howe), and wage labor on the mainland—without threatening the continuity of the household as a subsistence unit. Second, as we have seen among the Miskito and the Black Caribs, the consanguineally related women within the matrilocal extended family provide a core of protective solidarity for the family, particularly when men are away. Third, older men (fathers-in-law) are still able to exert various forms of pressure on younger men (sons-in-law), maintaining a measure of traditional respect and obligation.

Holloman's findings suggest interesting contrasts with the Miskito of eastern Nicaragua. Miskito data from the village of Asang (Helms 1971) indicate that most households contain a single nuclear family or a nuclear family with

131

assorted individual relatives. However, residence close to the home of the wife's parents and growing village endogamy make it possible for consanguineally related women to support and assist each other in a range of household and agricultural activities. In the absence of extended families the roles of father-in-law and sons-in-law appear to be more loosely expressed than among the Cuna, although mutual aid and assistance is expected in house building, pig butchering, and food sharing if one of the families runs short of its own provisions. This looser association of father-in-law and sons-in-law may well reflect the fact that day-to-day agricultural work among the Miskito has traditionally been the women's chore, while men individually (or perhaps with a friend or relative) hunted, fished, and sought jobs with foreign concerns. There has been no area of men's activities requiring strongly cooperative efforts between father- and sons-in-law or strong control and direction of sons-in-law by fathers-in-law for an extended period of time. Matrilocal tendencies among the Miskito, therefore, reflect the second factor noted by Holloman (social solidarity provided by cores of related women), together with that portion of her first point stressing the viability of the matrilocally affiliated group as a subsistence unit (in the Miskito case, this reflects women's responsibility and mutual assistance in agriculture rather than men's activities).

The major contrast, then, between Cuna and Miskito is found in the ideal and tradition of long-term control of sons-in-law by fathers-in-law among the Cuna and the apparent absence of this strong association and direction among Miskito men. The source of this contrast may lie in the pre-Columbian social organizations of eastern Nicaraguan tribes and Panamanian chiefdoms, respectively. To the best of our knowledge the pre-Columbian ancestors of the Miskito were seminomadic egalitarian tribesmen with a division of labor whereby adult men hunted and fished more or less individually (judging from technology and contact accounts) while women were responsible for agriculture. The ancestors of the Cuna, however, were members of hierarchically ranked chiefdoms where men apparently were more involved in agricultural activities and where chiefs and members of the ruling elite probably relied strongly for the attainment of their political goals on assistance from groups of supporters. Some of these supporters, the historical documents suggest, were sons-in-law and fathers-in-law.* The reader will recall, too, that Young's chapter on the significance of the krun *among the western Guaymí evidences the importance of groups of men in native Panamanian society. The major*

---

*Holloman notes that the Cuna word for father-in-law or mother-in-law is saka, *a term which Stout (1947: 81) suggests may well derive from the pre-Columbian term* saka *or* saco; *as we mentioned in the headnote to the first essay in this volume, this is also the term accorded a level of Panamanian elite by the Spanish chroniclers. In the pre-Columbian era high-status* sacos *were probably also allied as sons- and fathers-in-law to each other and to the* quevi, *or high chief, who frequently had many wives.*

participants of krun, *the host and his ritual partner, are "men of importance" who rely heavily on groups of supporters for the resources necessary to stage* krun. *In short, Panamanian materials yield evidence from several quarters indicating a definite place and function in society, past and present, for units composed of a "man of authority" and his supporters. The materials for eastern Nicaragua do not indicate any comparable association between groups of men. The difference in household forms observed between Cuna and Miskito today may be due at least in part to this basic contrast. The fact that both groups have developed matrilocal residence patterns reflects the usefulness of this adaptation (particularly the solidarity of groups of related women) in post-contact experiences.*

Among the world's nonurban, nonstate peoples the San Blas Cuna of Panama have been unusually successful in adapting to changes associated with their incorporation into the world market system and into the political and economic life of the Republic of Panama. The extent of developmental change in San Blas since 1900 is strikingly apparent in the spread of literacy and bilingualism, the development of a small native middle class, and the achievement of confederal union by the numerous local community-chieftaincies (Holloman 1969). The normative male life cycle now includes multiple periods of living and working in the cities of Panama, in the Canal Zone, or (less likely) in one of the agribusinesses operated in Panama by foreign corporations. Yet, despite these extensive changes in aspects of life which are functionally related to family and household organization, Cuna household organization in 1967, the date of the field work upon which this report is based, remained relatively traditional.

At that date, well beyond the time when disorganization or transformation of the matrilocal domestic units might have been predicted, most Cuna households were not only viable units but appeared to be absorbing much of the stress created in other areas of social life. Deviation from approved cultural forms of residence was extremely limited in all but a few villages. Where significant modification of traditional forms was found, the change was not recent but was associated with radical modernization programs adopted by a few towns in the first quarter of this century. The continuity in household structure was *not*, however, paralleled by a similar conservatism in attitude. Of 30 male informants under the age of 35, none saw matrilocality as *personally* desirable, although several connected the matrilocal household with the good of the community as a whole. Over half favored neolocality as a replacement norm, yet only one man was actually living neolocally. Other segments of the population—men and women over 35 and women 35 and under—favored the traditional norm.

The vitality of the traditional household over a sixty-five-year period of rapid socioeconomic change and the discrepancy between attitudes and behavior in one segment of the present population raise questions about the manner in which readaptation occurs in a functionally vital area of a traditional social system. It is my purpose in this chapter to show that the apparent structural continuity in San Blas household organization masks important changes in the actual roles of the members of the unit. The Cuna matrilocal household has indeed provided one of the points of flexibility and strength in the readaptation of the social system as a whole. This has been so because it has been possible to redistribute labor within the unit while preserving, at least for a time, the relative prestige of its various members. In 1967 the structuring of the key father-in-law/son-in-law dyad had two sometimes disparate aspects: actual task performance and deference behavior. For the most part sons-in-law continued to display at least surface respect to their fathers-in-law, but the manner in which male work activities were carried out and the time budgets of older and younger males had altered markedly. Finally, although a number of change-associated processes were undercutting the traditional structure, a new reinforcement process had developed.

The Household Survey

In the sections that follow data are presented on household organization in 29 households in the community of San Ignacio de Tupile in 1967. The data are examined first to establish the traditional norms for the domestic cycle and then with an eye to what changes in key roles and dyads they reflect. The points of tolerance and of stress in the traditional and the adapted systems are examined.

The sample upon which the study is based was assembled judgmentally, because the purpose of the survey was to establish the total range of variation in household form and function, not to obtain a representative sample for purposes of extrapolation. I assumed that occupation, sex, educational background, age, relative power and prestige, attitude toward change, and idiosyncratic (personality and background) factors would all be variables. Since Cuna communities are endogamous and, in fact, only a handful of Tupile residents had been born elsewhere, place of origin was not a variable. After I had

assembled a sample of 25 on this basis I consulted with Cuna informants, who suggested four additional households on the basis that
they were "different" in one way or another. It is highly unlikely that
there were styles of family organization on Tupile at the time of the
study which are not represented in the findings. Because of the nature of the sample, however, the n's for the various types of household
should not be regarded as representative of their distribution in the
community as a whole. The same is true with respect to average
household size. Range for the sample was from five to fourteen, with
an average of eight; this may or may not represent the community
average. I estimate that the sample represented about 20 percent
of all households in the community (population about 1200).

Defining "household" for the purposes of the survey proved to
be the first task of research. The emic approach to household definition would have been based on the attitude "is responsible for." Any
adult in the community could have declared any other person a
member of so-and-so's household, meaning that that household head
was nominally responsible to the village for the conduct of that individual. This definition was not suitable for my purposes since younger
men who were definitely not functional members of a given household might under certain conditions of interpersonal conflict be regarded by the village as under the jurisdiction of the older male head
of that household. The definition of household which I finally arrived
at rested upon degree of use of a common kitchen. A Cuna household
in this sense is a group of affinally, consanguineally, and/or adoptively
related individuals who eat together in a common kitchen for most
meals.

Traditional Cuna domestic architecture comprises two sorts of
structures: sleeping huts and kitchens. The kitchen hut is somewhat
the smaller. Both are oval and are constructed of cane with palm
thatch. One or more sleeping huts may be associated with each
household unit. The existence of a separate kitchen does not necessarily imply a separate household, although it *is* a sign that the process of
household division is under way. The junior unit may not become
fully independent for many years. As a result, neither a simple count
of sleeping huts nor one of kitchens can be used to ascertain the total
number of households in a San Blas community. The 29 households
included in the survey comprised 36 sleeping huts and 31 kitchens. In
a multi-hut unit the second sleeping hut is ideally constructed next to
the principal hut, but it may be located at a considerable distance from
the main unit and the common kitchen.

A further caution is necessary before the data are presented. This has to do with the assumption that the situation on San Ignacio de Tupile is broadly representative of San Blas as a whole. It has already been stated that several villages are notable for having taken an early position in favor of radical modernization. The nuclear family predominates in these communities and houses there are considerably smaller. There is also at least one possible traditional variant. In a number of communities which lie at the end of the archipelago nearest to Colombia the houses are noticeably larger than those on Tupile and are often built in compound style with a surrounding fence or with a fence joining the principal structures. How this visible difference is reflected in household organization is unknown, but there must be correlates. Other variations by community may also exist.

Important for understanding the conditions on Tupile is the saturation of living space. Every available house site was occupied in 1967. This is true for many other communities but not for all. For example, Howe (1974) found some neolocality on Tikantiki where there still is vacant land, confirming my impression that the presence or absence of land for an independent house site is a significant factor affecting postmarital residence patterns. There has as yet been no in-depth survey of such differences in San Blas. I would predict that frequencies of household types will be found to vary from one community to the next and that this sort of information will be extremely useful for an understanding of some of the internal processes which give the various communities their distinctiveness.

The Normative Domestic Cycle

Throughout San Blas, with the exception of those communities which have a long history of identification with the concept of modernity, the norm of household composition and development is the same: a father-in-law and a mother-in-law (in Spanish, *suegro* and *suegra;* in Cuna, *saka* for both) head a household, all of whose members live in a house which she owns. The other members are one or more daughters, with their husbands and children, and any unmarried sons. The men of the household comprise an agricultural work team under the direction of the father-in-law. Ideally, the household grows and prospers so that the sleeping hut becomes crowded and a second sleeping hut must be built. The women of this multi-hut unit continue to pool their labor, the male work team remains intact, and all members of the household eat in the joint kitchen. With the death of the older couple the eldest daughter inherits the house and her husband becomes the male head-of-household.

I have described the norms of household organization along the axis of affinity because this is the way the Cuna see their households in most contexts. It is a male-oriented view and the key relationship in terms of the household's growth and prosperity is that between the in-married male head and his in-married sons-in-law. The most important functional attribute of the Cuna household is that it is the unit of subsistence production, and agricultural work organization is based upon relationships among males. Unmarried men work under the direction of their fathers. After marriage the obligation to fathers and brothers is secondary to that to the father-in-law. A man asks permission of his father-in-law when he wants to spend a day working with his father. What is involved is a period of bride service which lasts until the death of the older man, or until he agrees to an earlier termination of the obligations involved.

If the mother-in-law dies first the traditional system is embarrassed. The norms do not really provide for this eventuality, since it brings into conflict the principles of female ownership of the house and male obligation to bride service to the father-in-law. The father-in-law becomes a visitor in his own house. Generally he remarries quickly and moves out. This releases the sons-in-law. The household may then split or it may remain together under the eldest of the brothers-in-law, a cobrothers-in-law form.

The norms do provide for a number of commonly occurring eventualities, most of them centering upon irregularities in the father-in-law/son-in-law relationship. When a man marries a woman whose father is already dead, the young man is under no obligation to reside uxorilocally unless he is the only son-in-law. In this case he moves into his wife's household and his status is that of senior male, although if he is young or timid the household may be completely dominated by the mother-in-law. Sons-in-law have no obligation to stepfathers-in-law regardless of when the marriage was contracted. A final adjustment permits the adoption or borrowing of children by barren couples. The child is typically a niece or nephew and is given "out of love" of one adult sibling for another.

Severe conflict between parents and son-in-law in the early stages of marriage usually results in divorce. In the later stages of a marriage it is one of the common factors leading to the fission of a multi-unit household.

Earlier accounts of the Cuna household have fixed upon the ownership of the house by females and the subsequent continuity over time of the household through a female line. Stout, for example, states that "In short, it [the household] is a group of conjugal units united through marriage to a lineage of women" (1947: 25). This statement is formally correct if we understand "lineage" to refer to a principle of descent and not to an organized kin group. No activities or groupings outside the household are organized in terms of a female lineage principle.

However, when the Cuna talk about their households they usually take the female principle for granted. The household is to them a way of organizing unrelated men into work units and of coordinating these units into the broader community structure under its chiefs and *voceros* or speakers. Ownership of the house through females is a complementary but more restricted theme. This is not to say that it is unimportant. Cuna women are expected to be strong personalities; the colorful, domineering mother-in-law figure is important in joking and in actual household continuity.[1] But to understand the way in which the domestic cycle has been and is being altered, one must look to men and their relationships and activities.

The normative cycle accounts for the following types of household: the prototypical household headed by a father-in-law and mother-in-law, all members living in one sleeping hut; a large version of the same household whose members live in more than one sleeping hut, but share a kitchen; the mother-in-law-headed household with the position of male head-of-household filled by the eldest son-in-law; a cobrothers-in-law (in Spanish, *concuñado*) household (the remnant of the prototype after the death of the parents-in-law). The norms also account for a type of patrilocality—the presence within the household of a son and daughter-in-law under certain circumstances (when the son's father-in-law has died and he is neither married to the eldest daughter nor the only son-in-law); for the presence of nonlineally related (borrowed) children; for returned sons (men divorced or separated); for a widowed or separated brother (usually of the mother-in-law); and for the absence of *acudiente* children (those working for room and board in a home on the mainland) and of males engaged in wage labor on the mainland.

The survey included three household types regarded as deviations by those subscribing to traditional norms: a neolocal kind; a matrilocal household with a patrilocal component *not* explainable by the norm described above; and (most important) what I term the "absentee son-in-law" household—a type with at least one married daughter with dependents but no resident son-in-law. In this last type of household the roles of the father-in-law and the son-in-law with respect to agricultural labor are inverted. The father-in-law, instead of having a son-in-law to help, works harder than before in order to support his son-in-law's dependents.

The complete system as it applies to households in the Tupile sample is described in the following sections. Diagrams of the household types are presented in Figure 1.[2]

A.1 THE PROTOTYPE SUEGRO HOUSEHOLD

The first type of household, the prototype of the *suegro* (father-in-law) kind, involves a single sleeping hut shared by at least two nuclear families, one the *suegro-suegra* family and the second the daughter of this couple and their son-in-law. Also in the house will be unmarried children of both couples. Frequently there is a married son separated or divorced from his wife and a widowed or separated sister or brother of the mother-in-law (the debris of a dissolved household).

In the Tupile sample eight households were classified as of this type. Two of these contained members of three adult generations. That is, an A.2 *suegra*-headed household had persisted and with the marriage of a granddaughter the old *suegra*, still living, was retired. In one household the *suegro* and *suegra* were childless and the younger couple was the *suegra*'s niece and her husband. This was an example of a borrowed child. There was a second such child (male), not yet of marriageable age, in this same household.

A.2 THE SUEGRA HOUSEHOLD

In the second form, the *suegra* household, there is a single sleeping hut with the mother-in-law and at least one married daughter and son-in-law present. Five of the households in the sample were of this type. In three cases there was a step-*suegro* present, but the sons-in-law were not obligated to work under his direction. In one case the step-*suegro* and the stepson-in-law were both vigorous and had established a cooperative work relationship on a friendship basis. In the two other cases the step-*suegro* was clearly living in "her" house with "her" children. One of these latter men had been an extremely influential man in the community in his prime and was the object of considerable respect in his retirement. This did not, however, carry over to his relationship within the household to his wife's children. The work on his numerous farm plots was done by his sons, the old man being beyond the age for agricultural work. The weak position of the step-

Figure 1   Household Types on the Island of San Ignacio de Tupile
($n = 29$)

A.1 Prototype: The *Suegro* (Father-in-Law) Household (n = 8)

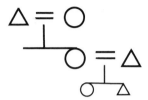

A.2 The *Suegra* (Mother-in-Law) Household: original father-in-law deceased or divorced; household headed by mother-in-law, with or without stepfather-in-law (n = 5)

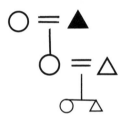

A.3 The *Concuñado* (Cobrothers-in-Law) Household (n = 3)

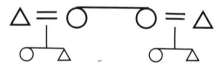

A.4 The Absentee *Yerno* (Son-in-Law) Household (n = 5)

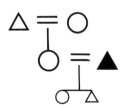

Figure 1 (Continued)

B.1 Prototype: The Common Kitchen Household ($n = 5$)

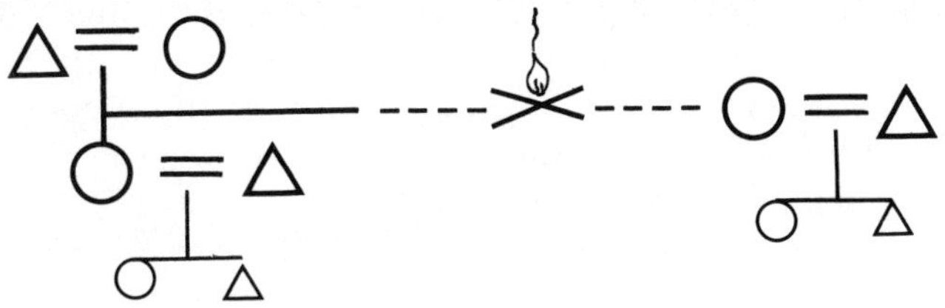

B.2 The Common Kitchen Household with Patrilocality ($n = 2$)

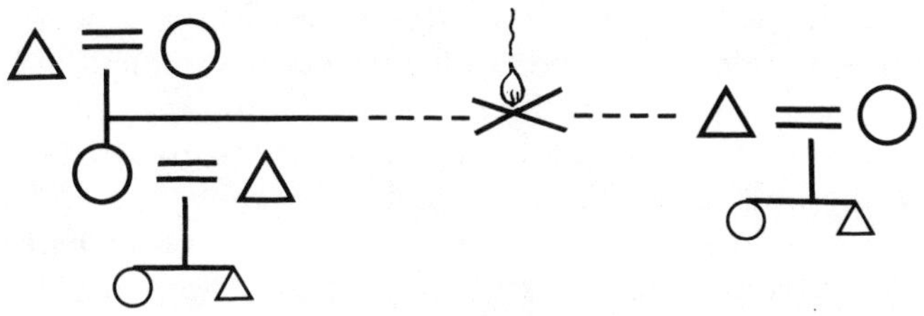

C The Independent Conjugal Household ($n = 1$)

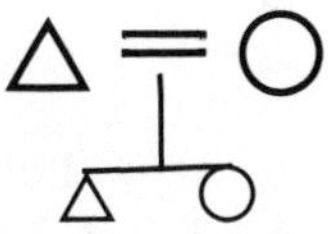

---

suegro in most households comes from the fact that the younger men in the house know that their wives and eventually their children will inherit nothing from this man. (Inheritance among the Cuna is bilateral and land is owned separately by husband and wife.) In *suegra*-headed households, whether the *suegra* is actually the household head is a function of her personality. Many older Cuna women are capable of dominating such a situation.

A.3 THE CONCUÑADO HOUSEHOLD

The *concuñado* household is based on two or more sisters and their husbands. The older generation is deceased but the brothers-in-law have elected to preserve the joint household. The eldest is household head. Three of the households in the sample were of this type. In two cases the *suegra* was deceased and the *suegro* had remarried and was living in another household. In the third case both *suegro* and *suegra* were deceased, as was the wife of one of the brothers-in-law. This last household contained only one intact nuclear family; the widowed brother-in-law was a full-time agriculturalist and the other had considerable income from nonagricultural activities—examples of a kind of symbiotic relationship produced by the fact that there was no buying and selling of subsistence commodities on the island at the time of the study.

A.4 THE ABSENTEE YERNO HOUSEHOLD

An absentee *yerno* (son-in-law) household was one in which there were *no* sons-in-law present, generally because the husbands of all married daughters were working outside the San Blas region. There were five of these households in the sample. Nine households in all had at least one member working outside San Blas at the time of the study, but in these five cases there was no younger man present. This occurred most often when a man had only one daughter. Periodic wage labor in mainland Panama is a part of the adult male life cycle. It is an accepted Cuna device for augmenting cash income and/or procuring expensive items such as sewing machines, beds, guns, and motors. In these five households the pattern had been pushed to an extreme which undercut the traditional relationship between father-in-law and son-in-law. In effect, an older agriculturalist was left to feed a large number of dependent females and children. The average household size of these five was 7.4, very little under the average of 8 for the sample as a whole. The physical strain of the work involved showed on the faces of the fathers-in-law, who, at the age of 50 to 55, should (according to the traditional value system) have been beginning to relax and leave the heaviest work to their sons-in-law. In only one case was the situation regarded by the *suegro* as acceptable on a permanent basis. The man's only daughter had been married for ten years to a man who had worked at a good job with PanCanal for twenty-five years. The entire household went to Panama once or twice a year to visit him and he visited his wife and children three or four times a year. He sent regular support to the household. What permitted the pattern in this case was the extremely good wages paid for his particular job and the responsible attitude of the son-in-law.

B.1 THE PROTOTYPE COMMON KITCHEN HOUSEHOLD

In the common kitchen household a family with two or more sleeping huts shares a single kitchen (pooled female labor). There may or may not be labor-pooling among the men eating in the joint kitchen. Five households were in this category. The five are a mixed group because this household type has served traditionally as a convenient social fiction for A.1 household growth, division, and breakup. Often the taking of meals in common is irregular and the houses are connected only because the persons involved and the village do not choose to acknowledge their separateness. The Cuna have a developed and culturally important shame or loss-of-face concept (Cuna, *pinge;* Spanish, *peina*); inability to hold a household together is a source of *suegro* shame. In only two cases were all the secondary sleeping huts involved in the joint kitchen actually adjacent to the *suegro*'s hut. In one case, for example, the main hut was located in the center of the island. A second hut, built by a 35-year-old son-in-law for his nuclear family, was on the tip of the island on land owned by the wife's relatives. This nuclear family ate daily in the joint kitchen. The young man stated that it had taken him four years to obtain his *suegro*'s permission to move out of the main hut and the cooperative work group. He felt himself to be living neolocally but diplomatically with respect to both the community mores and the feelings of his *suegro* (who was one of the most important men in the town).

B.2 THE COMMON KITCHEN HOUSEHOLD WITH PATRILOCAL UNIT

Two of the common kitchen households contained a new element related by those involved to acculturative change. The main hut in both cases was of the traditional A.1 type. The second hut in each case contained a son and daughter-in-law of the male head-of-household, and the secondary hut was constructed on land owned by *his* parents, not hers. In one case the son was a teacher in the school and the girl newly returned from a long period as *acudiente*. She wore modern dress and did not speak Cuna. The second case was similar. The acculturated son of an otherwise traditional family was living in a cement house he had built on land owned by one of his relatives. This man had attended Artes y Officios, a trade school in Panama. He was a carpenter and builder and he and his wife and children had returned from a two-year stay in Panama six months prior to my arrival. In both of these cases the acculturated households were not independent because they had no kitchen huts; all meals were taken in the household of origin of the husband. The parents or other relatives of the husband had made possible the deviation by providing a house site.

Stout describes a multi-hut unit which he calls "related households" (1947: 28). Such houses, he says, may be related through the women (in which case the unit fits what I have called the common kitchen category) or they may be affinally related, the son of one being married to the daughter of the other. Stout states that such related households not only pool labor but use a common burial ground. The idea of households which were unrelated consanguineally sharing a common burial ground was unknown on Tupile. It may be that Stout's data record a variation of traditional practice found in the communities in which he worked (probably Ailigandi or Ustupu), or it may be that the households involved were consanguineally related in a way unknown to him. Given village endogamy, this is likely to be the case.

C THE INDEPENDENT CONJUGAL HOUSEHOLD

The independent conjugal variety of household is neolocal, contains only one conjugal unit, has its own kitchen hut, and is in general completely separate from the household of either set of parents or siblings. Only one household in the survey met these criteria. This was the household of a man of about 30 who had worked in Panama for a number of years. His wife had also lived in Panama and wore modern dress. He worked in agriculture but spent about three days per week as a professional fisherman. The land for his house site had been planted with coconuts and was one of the last available sites of this sort on the island. The land had been owned jointly by his paternal relatives. The decision to give this young man the house site was made after long discussions by the entire group of patrilateral kin—in this case the surviving children of his paternal grandfather and their children, all of whom had nominal claims to the income from the coconut trees on the land.[3]

The Traditional Household as an Adaptive System Under Conditions of Male Role Change

Of the many changes in Cuna life in this century the one which has had the most far-reaching consequences is the change in the work role of males. At the time of my field work very few men in the age range 18 to 35 were resident on Tupile. Most of these had recently come from working on the mainland or were anticipating their next period of wage labor there. This pattern began to develop in the 1930s when large numbers of men began to work in the Canal Zone and in mainland Panama.[4] It was accelerated by the labor shortage during World War II and by the economic boom after the war. The commitment of the Cuna to this altered male life cycle introduced functionally related pressure for replacement of traditional education by modern schooling. So the man who was between the ages of 18 and 35 at the time of the study differed from his elders in more than one way.

In 1967 the young man who had no desire to leave San Blas to work on the mainland was deviant. On the other hand, none of those interviewed was considering the possibility of *permanent* residence outside San Blas. The expectation of a young man growing up at the time of the study was that he would marry a Cuna woman, have children, and leave his family in his native village during his periodic work-related absences. Although he would have preferred to build his own house and live neolocally, he recognized that this would be difficult and that his wife, at any rate, would prefer to remain with her family during his absences.

Because he intended eventually to retire to his home community, the absent worker was careful to fulfil at least minimum work obligations to his own brothers and father to prevent the lapsing of his land inheritance rights. Since he could not perform his share of the labor on family land he contributed money or goods instead. He was less likely to meet his labor obligations to his father-in-law because he knew that his children's inheritance through their mother would not be affected by his irresponsibility. (Abandonment and divorce were frequent at the time of the study, but there was indication that fragility in husband-wife bonding had been a part of Cuna social life for at least two generations.[5])

This, then, is the picture of Tupile households in 1967: traditional forms predominated, but new forms and new functions were clearly in evidence. Although complaining about the lack of industriousness of young men was the favorite conversational pastime of older men and considerable stress on household organization and marriage was in evidence, Tupile household structure was intact and supportive of its members in 1967.

I see three types of factors involved in the adaptive process at the household level. First, the traditional agricultural work unit of the Cuna, based as it was on the matrilocal extended family, was "underemployed." That is, the number of hours of agricultural labor per week required from the men of the average household to support themselves and their dependents was low enough so that each man had considerable spare time. (This time was put into cash cropping of coconuts, into political participation, and, in some communities, into an elaborate system of community organization and labor pooling.) It is not possible to estimate the time spent on agricultural labor by the average man in the period before a significant number of men were removed from the subsistence labor force, but I can give a rough estimate of the number of dependents an experienced farmer working 40 to 50 hours a week was able to support. My Cuna landlord was the head of one of the absentee son-in-law households in the study. The son-in-law was deceased; a grandson-in-law was working in Panama City. The grandfather was able to feed himself and seven dependents (two of them small children) almost entirely by his own labor. (A 15-year-old grandson worked with him sometimes on the weekends.)

A second factor is that the matrilocal extended family is an ideal unit for the support of women and children under conditions of absence of young fathers. Miller (1967), working among the Toba of Argentina, noted a similar functional link, as did Helms (1970) in her analysis of the adaptive significance of matrilocality among the Apache, the Miskito of eastern Nicaragua, and the Mbayá of

Paraguay. Both concluded that where matrilocality exists it is reinforced by a pattern of migratory labor for men. The Cuna extended family clearly is functioning to buffer women and children from the full psychological and economic consequences of male absenteeism.

Third, because of the nature of land tenure and of political power and because of the general lag in female acculturation relative to that of males, older men in 1967 still had several means available by which to exert pressure on younger men. The strength of these traditional controls prevented an abrupt collapse or reversal of the older man/younger man equation. On the other hand, attempts by the older men to extend traditional social controls into the cities failed. Voluntary associations formed on a community basis in Colón and Panama City were not under the control of the town government.[6] Once out of the region a man was subject only to family pressures and these were effective only with respect to his family of orientation.

Conclusion

Since Goody's statement on the matter it has been customary in anthropology to treat household organization dynamically, as a cyclic process of formation, development, and dissolution (Goody 1958). Conceiving the structure of domestic units as a series of states over time allows us to relate the several forms actually observed to identifiable social and biological processes, and to account for both conformity and deviation from norms within the framework of available strategies and individual choices. Linear processes of change can also be observed by collecting data on the cycle at various points in time, measuring changes in frequencies of alternate forms, and noting the introduction of new variants.

One of the oldest and knottiest problems in anthropology has to do with the search for predictable relationships between the household as an organizational unit and other sociocultural and ecological variables. Lévi-Strauss has been the foremost advocate of the idea that both house and village, as arrangements in space, can be actualizations of aspects of the symbolic code which underlies the social system (1967). Howe found this to be the case with the Cuna. The structure of the traditional Cuna house—overall form, parts, and materials—is used metaphorically to iterate important aspects of the Cuna sociopolitical order (Howe 1972). Others have examined household organization as a function of institutional and/or ecological variables.

One of the strongest connections cited by Murdock (1949) is that between work organization (with its associated technology) and post-marital residence. Although most of Murdock's cases concern pre-modern work situations, the Cuna data suggest that the association holds as well for migratory labor patterns under conditions of urbanization and industrialization. A migratory pattern of employment for males does indeed seem to reinforce matrilocality in a situation in which acculturative forces have already produced attitude change favoring neolocality.

Industrialization proceeds by tapping the underemployed rural labor force, just as agriculture in its turn tapped the even more extensive unused human energy potential at the hunting and gathering level. The pattern of concomitant changes associated with the transition, however, must be understood at the level of multiple possibilities rather than in unilinear fashion, as Eisenstadt has recently pointed out in his review of the naivetés of early modernization studies (1973). Urbanization and industrialization *are* highly constraining processes but they are not deterministic. The Cuna case, where the household is the unit of subsistence production, suggests that the key relationship may well be that between the constraints of the particular subsistence system and the organization of the complete set of household roles. That is, although matrilocality is functional under conditions of male absence, this factor *alone* is insufficient to explain the stability of the household system. The *fundamental* factor is surely the capacity of the traditional household to continue as a successful subsistence unit despite the sharp reduction of available male labor within the units. The traditional Cuna system had a range of tolerance sufficient to absorb early-stage stresses introduced by the changes in the male work pattern.

Notes

1. A study of the role of women in Cuna society has yet to be made. Like most female anthropologists until very recently, I concentrated on male-dominated aspects of Cuna life.

2. Interviews were conducted in Spanish, using a bilingual member of the household as translator in each case. The terms used in the typology are consequently Spanish, not Cuna. The overall level of bilingualism on Tupile was approximately 50 percent.

3. Cf. Howe's essay in this volume.

4. There was precedent for the absentee male pattern: in preceding centuries

the Cuna served as sailors on foreign sailing vessels. *How,* exactly, the present wage labor pattern affects the young men *themselves* has yet to be studied, although it is clear that physical separation from the villages, possession of an independent source of income, and association with other young Cuna in an extracultural setting must have feedbacks on the individuals and on their assorted social relationships.

5. One change occurred in the early part of the century which may have been crucial to marital stability under conditions of matrilocality: the average age at marriage rose. Marriage formerly occurred within a year after female puberty to males of the same age. This meant that at one time a man grew to maturity in the house of his father-in-law; this would have made the relationship more like that between father and son.

6. The traditional power structure was more successful in controlling internal mobility and right of egress. To go from his home village to another island an individual required a pass bearing the official seal of his village chief. Exit by air and by boat from the region was similarly controlled. My landlord stated that the next time his grandson-in-law returned he would ask the chief to refuse him permission to go back to Panama. These various sources of power supported the prestige and self-images of the traditional heads-of-household during a transitional period when agriculture as an occupation was losing prestige relative to urban wage labor.

References

Eisenstadt, S. N., 1973. *Tradition, Change and Modernity.* New York: Wiley-Interscience.

Goody, Jack, 1958. *The Developmental Cycle in Domestic Groups.* Cambridge Papers in Social Anthropology, No. 1. Cambridge, Eng.: Cambridge University Press.

Helms, Mary W., 1970. Matrilocality, social solidarity, and culture contact: three case histories. *Southwestern Journal of Anthropology,* 26: 197–212.

———, 1971. *Asang: Adaptations to Culture Contact in a Miskito Community.* Gainesville: University of Florida Press.

Holloman, Regina E., 1969. Developmental changes in San Blas. Ph.D. dissertation, Northwestern University.

Howe, James, 1972. Carrying the village: Cuna political metaphors. Unpublished manuscript.

———, 1974. Village political organization among the San Blas Cuna. Ph.D. dissertation, University of Pennsylvania.

Lévi-Strauss, Claude, 1967. *Structural Anthropology.* New York: Anchor.

Miller, Elmer S., 1967. Pentecostalism among the Argentine Toba. Ph.D. dissertation, University of Pittsburgh.

Murdock, George, 1949. *Social Structure.* New York: Macmillan.

Stout, David, 1947. *San Blas Cuna Acculturation: An Introduction.* Viking Fund Publications in Anthropology, No. 9. New York: Wenner-Gren Foundation for Anthropological Research.

Communal Land Tenure and the Origin
of Descent Groups Among the San Blas Cuna

JAMES HOWE

The following essay by James Howe describes yet another adaptation to frontier economic conditions in the Caribbean lowlands of lower Central America: the development of land-holding corporations among the San Blas Cuna as a means of exploiting cash-crop coconut groves under conditions of population growth that have led to increasing fragmentation of agricultural lands inherited individually. Howe describes in some detail the various ways in which corporate control of coconut groves provides the most efficient method of harvesting the nuts, and he shows how the various members of the corporation, who are also related by descent from the original owner of the grove, take turns harvesting and selling the ripe coconuts.

As Howe indicates, other examples of property-controlling "descent groups" may be found in the West Indies and also among the Black Caribs. There, too, population pressure on land and other inheritable resources (money, tools, residence sites) results in fragmentation and dispersal of resources, in the absence of primogeniture, ultimogeniture, or other such guidelines for inheritance (Solien 1959). To date there is no recorded evidence of comparable property-controlling kin groups for the Miskito, whose frontier adaptations are similar in many ways to those of the Black Caribs and the Cuna. However, goods such as saws, axes, sewing machines, guns, and dugout canoes that cannot be literally divided among the children or siblings of the deceased may be placed under the guardianship of one heir and freely borrowed as needed by the others (Helms 1971: 164). This procedure, in fact, appears not unlike the process used on a larger scale by the Cuna for coconut groves, for access to groves is a type of periodic use of indivisible property held in guardianship for all those involved by the oldest male of the oldest surviving generation descended from the original grove owner.

151

Howe's provocative discussion of the Cuna coconut-grove corporation in terms of descent-group theory broaches another "frontier" of anthropological study with implications far beyond Central America.

This chapter examines one aspect of land tenure among the San Blas Cuna, a population of some 25,000 agriculturists and fishermen inhabiting a set of island and shore villages strung out along the coast of northeastern Panama. The essay takes the position that certain kinds of joint tenure characteristic of the Cuna have led to the formation of descent-based corporations and that these groups have significant implications for general theories concerning kinship.[1]

Cuna Land Tenure

The Cuna say that just a few generations ago private property in land did not exist among them (cf. Nordenskiöld 1938: 40–41).[2] Fields cleared for slash-and-burn cultivation returned to the public domain within a few years when the users let them go fallow. At some time in the mid or late nineteenth century the landholding system changed. This change occurred along with, and according to informants was caused by, an increase in the San Blas Cuna population (which in turn resulted in increased pressure on agricultural land) and a great expansion in the cash-cropping of coconuts. Today, once a man has cleared a piece of forest it becomes his to hold and to pass on to his heirs or sell if he wishes. Unclaimed land still exists in most parts of San Blas, but only at considerable distances from the coast and from the shore and island villages. Many men continue to acquire some land by clearing it themselves, but typically they gain a large part of their holdings (and usually their most productive and accessible fields) through inheritance.

Only men clear land, so the original owner of a field is always a male, but inheritance is bilateral. Both sons and daughters inherit and in approximately equal proportions. Spouses do not inherit land from each other and their holdings are never formally merged as one estate, but husbands act as their wives' stewards by managing and exploiting their fields along with their own, and when speaking informally a man often describes his wife's fields as "mine" (*ankat*).

Typically adult children are given land gradually over a period of years. If their parents live to an old age, the children often acquire a large part, though seldom all, of their inheritance before their parents' deaths. Frequently the first land they receive consists of fallow fields, which the son or the daughter's husband is expected to plant with coconuts; already-producing groves are loaned out to the children temporarily, to exploit for a day, a week, or a month. The final division of lands is usually planned out well ahead of time, and in some cases children may even be regularly exploiting plots earmarked for them without yet having taken over formal title. The Cuna consciously recognize this system of gradual inheritance not only as a way of giving children a stake early in life and as a device for the efficient exploitation of land, but also as a means by which the senior generation can maintain some degree of lifelong control over their children and their sons-in-law (Holloman 1969: 248).

Holdings are not concentrated. For a variety of reasons men tend to clear plots in several locations, and the typical mature adult owns quite a few fields scattered over a wide area. For example, one middle-aged couple owned or had rights to thirty-five plots spread out along approximately 40 kilometers of the San Blas coast.

Some pieces of land are passed on to one heir or divided up among several, but others are held in common by all of them and some such jointly owned plots may be kept undivided through several generations. In many cases land that passes into joint tenure has already been planted with coconuts, and when it has not the heirs very often intend to clear and plant the land with coconuts within a few years.

Co-heirs exploit their coconut groves in rotation, or as they put it, they "see" them "by months" (*niiki takke*). Each individual or each segment (see below) takes a month or two months in turn. During that period the party whose turn has come up may gather all the coconuts that fall to the ground. Nuts may not be picked out of the trees, because that would be poaching on the next month's harvest and thus equivalent to stealing. This system of rotation is possible because palms bear more or less continuously. They yield fewer nuts in the San Blas dry season from January through March, but they never cease bearing altogether, and the rotation is typically arranged so that over the long run no one is short-changed.

The oldest male sibling in the senior generation is usually the leader of the joint heirs, and he takes the initiative in making whatever plans and decisions are necessary. He can be overridden by the will of the majority, however, as is true of decision making in almost all domains of Cuna life. After the land has been cleared and planted the groves are largely self-managing, since the minimal maintenance they require can be handled by each heir during his or her month.

When asked why they "see" coconuts by month, the Cuna on my principal field site invariably replied that joint ownership and rotating exploitation allowed them to divide parental lands more equitably than any other method, and in that way they avoid jealousy and dissatisfaction. They claimed that it is impossible to keep co-heirs content if they are given whole plots of land exclusively, because individual plots vary markedly in size and quality and the number of pieces owned by a parent is seldom the same as, or an even multiple of, the number of children. It was pointed out that parents often compromise by giving a considerable number of plots individually to their children and leaving the remainder in joint ownership.

The Cuna seem to understand their own motives clearly and without self-deception. Certainly land tenure is not the only aspect of Cuna social organization that has been shaped by the readiness of all Cuna to stand up for their rights and complain if they feel slighted in comparison with their fellows. Joint tenure, however, has probably been shaped by other factors as well, including the following:

First, the Cuna express a general preference for communal efforts in many spheres of life, including cash-cropping. Cooperative societies with voluntary membership and even whole villages own and exploit groves. (For information on these modes of organization, which fall outside the scope of this chapter, see Holloman 1969, Howe 1974, and forthcoming works by Richard Costello.) One informant maintained that a group with a leader can exploit and maintain its groves more efficiently and get work done more quickly than could an individual. At the same time the Cuna harbor negative feelings about groups and leaders (Howe 1974), and they show a strong streak of individualism in several aspects of political and economic life. Given this ambivalence toward leadership and group activities, it is probably significant that family-owned groves require relatively few communal work sessions or nonroutine decisions once they are set up.

A second factor is that the Cuna have two basic economic goals in raising coconuts: long-term capital growth and security, and a regular source of cash. In terms of the latter goal, the two forms of land tenure have different virtues. Individually owned groves provide their owners with a continual flow of small amounts of cash which can be applied to daily expenses. Jointly owned groves provide each shareholder at intervals with sums that are often (but not always) larger. Some joint groves provide very large amounts by local standards, fifty or one hundred dollars or more in a single month, the co-owners' turns being spaced over wide intervals. The few individuals whose complete holdings I was able to record held groves under both kinds of tenure; in the language of capitalist investment, each had a balanced portfolio of groves.

Finally, joint tenure makes special sense given the fragmentation of land holdings in San Blas into a great many scattered plots, the nature of the coconut as a crop, and the methods used to exploit it. Coconuts fall continuously, and in most parts of San Blas the Cuna seldom pick nuts off the trees. Fallen nuts can remain on the ground for some time without spoiling and for many or most groves they are collected only every few days. The wider the intervals between collections, however, the greater the losses to animal predators such as crabs and squirrels and to human thieves. (Coconuts are very easy to steal, and once stolen, impossible to identify.) Rotating exploitation appears to allow the individual to concentrate his attention on a smaller number of groves at any given point in time. By not fragmenting his efforts as much as he would if he owned all his plots individually, he loses less of the total yield.

This advantage is especially notable for lands at a great distance from the owner's village. An individual who held as sole owner a number of groves located ten or fifteen sea miles from his home would find it difficult to visit them all with any regularity. From records of a few informants' holdings, as well as more general kinds of information, it appears that both sorts of grove are found close to villages, but groves held in joint tenure by family groups and cooperative societies predominate heavily in the more remote areas. Some of the groves lie on the numerous islands without permanent habitation in the western end of San Blas, many of which are a few miles offshore; families often go to live in these locations temporarily when their months come up, exploiting the comparatively rich aquatic resources near the islands as well as the coconut palms.

In the first generation in which a grove is held in joint tenure the allocation of months is simple: each sibling has one share, and turns are usually rotated in order of birth. In succeeding generations rights are allocated *per stirpes,* that is, each share is subdivided by the number of children of the shareholder.[3] Thus in the hypothetical example diagrammed in Figure 1, where two brothers have respectively two children and four children, each of the four children of brother B will get a chance to exploit the grove half as often as their Uncle A's two children.

Figure 1 First Hypothetical Coconut-Grove-Owning Group

The subdivision of shares is often handled by a system of minor rotation within major rotation. Turns rotate within the senior generation (whether living or dead), and each time the turn of a deceased member of that generation comes up it is given to a different one of his or her children. In the case of groves that have been held in joint tenure for several generations, rotation occurs at each generational level.[4] The ancestor who provides the point of focus for a segment within which subrotation takes place—the source of that segment's share—is known as the *nono* or "head" of the segment, and the eldest male of the senior living generation within a segment often represents him within the larger group.

A few examples are called for in order to clarify these remarks. The following examples, the first three including the set of kinsmen diagrammed in Figure 2, will also show some of the range of variation in the rotation arrangements.

1. Several groves are held jointly by the offspring of man A, who is deceased, and turns rotate among them. Each time the turn of L, who is also deceased, comes up, a different one of his three sons takes

Figure 2 Second Hypothetical Coconut-Grove-Owning Group

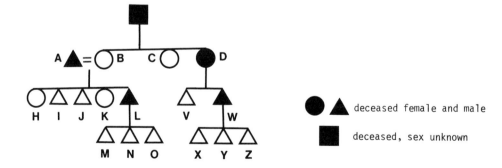

it. M, the eldest, represents his brothers, and L's share is sometimes spoken of as M's rather than as his father's.

2. A's wife B and her two sisters, one of whom is now dead, inherited another grove from one of their parents. Months rotate among them in three major shares. Every time the turn of D, the deceased sister, comes up, it goes to one or the other of her sons, V or W. Since W is also dead, his share rotates among *his* sons, X, Y, and Z. B, on the other hand, is living but she is very old and her eldest children are middle-aged. A different child takes her month each time it comes up and, as in the previous example, L's share rotates among his sons.

3. This same elderly woman, B, has rights in a large and productive island at some distance from her village. Rights to the grove there have already been subdivided for a few generations above her own, so there are a number of shares in her generation held by distantly related kinsmen from several different villages. Her turn comes up only every couple of years, and each time it does she gets two months. She has not passed on her rights in this grove permanently to her children, and she allocates their shares in an arrangement slightly different from the one discussed in the previous example. Every second time her turn comes up one daughter and one son, H and I, exploit the grove for one month and another pair, J and K, take the second month. Then, on alternate turns, she lets the children of her dead son, L, have two weeks, while she takes the other six. (In practice this means that during those six weeks someone exploits the grove in her behalf.)

4. In another arrangement (not illustrated by a diagram) six siblings hold a set of four groves. Each grove rotates by month among the six. On any given month four siblings are exploiting groves and two are sitting out.

These examples should make it clear that although certain general principles guide the allocation of rights, idiosyncratic variants occur frequently, and participants consciously plan out their own rotational systems.[5]

Descent Groups

Previous ethnographers of the Cuna have noted the presence of communal land tenure and rotating exploitation of coconut groves

(Nordenskiöld 1938: 40–41; Stout 1947: 24–25; and see especially Holloman 1969: 170–176). They have not pointed out, however, that the land-holding groups in fact constitute cognatic descent corporations. Membership in them derives from a rule of descent through males and/or females from a named ancestor, and they fit all of the criteria for corporations generally used in anthropology in that they act as individuals in some respects, they outlast their members, they hold common estates, and they have internal rules and leadership.

There are several reasons why it might not be immediately apparent that the land-holding groups are descent groups. In the past, kinship theory allowed only for the existence of unilineal descent groups; even in recent years, when many anthropologists have recognized the possibility of cognatic or nonunilineal descent groups, the tendency to think of descent groups as unilineal has persisted. The work of British social anthropologists also leads one to think of descent groups, where they are present in a tribal society, as *a* dominant or *the* dominant mode of organization, that which gives members of the society their primary social identity. For the Cuna this is clearly not the case since the groups exist only for a few specific functions and they are neither named nor extolled as groups by their members.[6] These characteristics do not disqualify them as descent groups, however, except to those like Fortes who deny the possibility of cognatic descent groups altogether.[7]

Anthropologists have repeatedly noted the destruction of descent groups by the introduction of a cash economy, incorporation into a nation-state, and other influences from the nontribal world (e.g., Gough 1961; Goodenough 1963), and studies of kinship among peasants and other members of complex societies tend to concentrate on domestic groupings and kinship networks. Here we have a case in which descent groups not only survived under modernizing influences but indeed first developed under them, since the Cuna land-holding groups are intimately involved with the coconut trade. The Cuna cannot be taken as typical in this respect, and ultimately the viability of their descent groups cannot be considered apart from their general success at preserving and even strengthening many communal aspects of their social organization; but their case does suggest that generalizations about the destruction or disappearance of descent groups deserve reexamination. It may be that if kinship groups, whether descent-based or not, are closely adapted to certain economic conditions they will not often survive a major change in these conditions. Further, kin-based groups that fulfill the same functions as centralized governments or other nonkinship organizations may be replaced or suppressed by them. On the other hand, limited-purpose descent groups may be adaptive even under new conditions, and because they are not always readily apparent to observers they may be frequently overlooked.

Cognatic land-holding groups may occur more often among peasants and other peoples on the margins of cash economies than is generally supposed. Solien (1959), for example, notes the presence of cognatic, or in her terms nonunilineal, descent groups among the Black Caribs of Honduras, and on the basis of more limited information from sources on Jamaica and Haiti she concludes that such groups probably occur widely throughout the Caribbean and Central America. Smith describes cognatic land-holding groups (as well as patrilineages with more diffuse functions) for Carriacou in the southeastern Caribbean (1962: 296), and in field work on Grand Cayman in the western Caribbean I also found cognatic land-holding groups.

It would not be surprising to discover similar groups in other parts of the world, since they provide a simple, straightforward mechanism for the management of property. They are adaptive wherever there are reasons to hold land or some other property intact (or at least a lack of motives for dividing it) and where both sexes are allowed to inherit rights in that property.

Ethnographers have often observed the decline of descent groups, but to date they have recorded very few, if any, instances of the beginnings of new descent systems, and this lack has rendered generalizations on this topic somewhat speculative. The notion that descent groups universally develop out of residence alignments has had wide currency, especially since Murdock made it a key element in his theory of the evolution of kinship (1949), but in the absence of documented cases this supposed sequence is in fact merely a plausible hypothesis. Goodenough has suggested that descent groups may arise in other ways (1963), and Scheffler has taken the more extreme position that the development of descent groups from residence groups "cannot be confirmed or disconfirmed and is of no scientific interest" (1973: 774). Nevertheless, many other authors continue to accept Murdock's position, either implicitly or explicitly (e.g., Aberle 1961: 659–660; Stephens 1963: 126–132; Fox 1967b: 86–92; Service 1971: 112–113).

The Cuna case, though limited in its applicability by its very uniqueness, at the very least destroys the universality of the

residence-to-descent sequence, since the Cuna descent groups develop out of a rule of inheritance rather than a rule of residence.
True, the groups in question are cognatic or bilateral and Murdock
had unilocal residence and unilineal descent in mind, but given a
mode of inheritance that favored one sex over the other the same
process could easily have produced unilineal descent groups. The
members of Cuna descent groups are never co-resident, apart from
the marginal exception of unmarried juvenile siblings living in their
parents' home, since the Cuna rule of residence is firmly matrilocal.
(See Holloman's chapter in this volume.) From the evidence of informants who were alive at the end of the nineteenth century, it seems
certain that residence was also matrilocal during the years in which
the descent groups first appeared.

The connection between the origin of descent groups and the
purposes they are to serve is indirect in Murdock's scheme: residence
alignments supposedly lead members to recognize a mode of group-
ing based on common ancestry, and this in turn is put to some use or
uses. The Cuna evidence lends support to Goodenough's alternative
suggestion that in many cases the relationship may be more direct: the
uses to which a group is to be put, whether mutual support and
protection, cooperative labor, or, as in this case, the preservation of
property in an undivided state, can play a direct part in promoting the
development of the group (Goodenough 1963: 925–928).

Groups, Purposes, and Descent Reckoning

A tendency has existed for a long time in "descent theory" or "lineage
theory" to take certain kinds of highly developed descent systems as
ideal types and to relate others to them. Those that do not fit are
identified as attenuated versions of the type or just ignored. It is, I
believe, much more productive to take into consideration a wide
range of forms in which ancestor-focus plays some part, including
instances where other organizational principles combine with it. In
this framework highly developed, multifunctional unilineal lineages
that provide their members with a large part of their primary social
identity take their place as just one variety (though obviously a very
significant one) of descent groups in general.

If it is accepted that Cuna land-holding groups qualify as descent
corporations, then they are interesting as an extreme or limiting case.
Rights to membership are entirely ascriptive—only descendants of the

founding ancestor can belong—but the decision whether to form a group, and later whether to dissolve it, is voluntary and consciously taken. Thus in some ways the groups fall on the borderline between kinship groups and voluntary societies.

As with many kinds of cognatic kinship group, a Cuna individual can belong to several. In fact some Cuna belong to quite a few, others to none at all, with the result that Cuna society is *not* divided up into a set of units of similar size and scale, an outcome that we tend to associate with descent systems. It has sometimes been argued that the overlap in membership of cognatic kinship groups renders them incapable of acting as corporations (Fortes 1969: 122–137, 276–308), a conclusion the Cuna groups clearly belie. A given Cuna individual may have rights in several different pieces of land, but the corporations controlling those plots are mutually exclusive. Indeed, in some cases in which the same set of people share the ownership of several different groves it could even be argued that they constitute a separate corporation in respect to each grove.

Cuna descent groups exist only for a few purposes, notably land holding and cash-cropping.[8] As such, they underline the point that in some cases it is less useful to characterize a whole society as patrilineal, matrilineal, or whatever, than it is to specify the total range of organizational arrangements found in the society and the uses to which each is put. In the Cuna case we can carry the point even further because the land-holding groups cannot be separated from their functions even in terms of their formal status as groups. A Cuna descent group exists as a distinct entity with boundaries that separate its members from other cognatically related kinsmen *only* because it possesses a piece of land. Cognatic kinship reckoning makes the members kinsmen, but the land makes them a descent group.[9]

Notes

1. This report derives from research carried out in San Blas during two field trips in 1970–1971 and 1971, respectively, supported by a research fellowship and field training grant from the National Institutes of Health.
2. In some cases descriptions of land tenure practices may offer a threat to the people whose practices are described. The broad outlines of Cuna land tenure have already been described, and at the moment Cuna lands are protected by the reservation status of San Blas. Should the situation change the new details offered here would not assist any outsiders in exploiting the Cuna or depriving them of their lands.

3. Richard Costello informs me that he found *per stirpes* division during his research (personal communication). Holloman, however, describes allocation of rights *per capita* (1969: 173). Costello and I worked on islands within a few miles of each other, while Holloman's primary field site was in another part of San Blas; the differences between her data and ours may derive, then, from regional variations.

4. Holloman has seen books used by the members of large land-holding groups to keep track of the order of rotation (personal communication).

5. I even recorded one case in which the two members of a sibling pair did not receive the same rights in communally held groves. For some groves the complete parental share was given to one sibling, for others it was given to the other sibling, and for still others the share was divided between them in the usual way. Siblings also sometimes sell their shares to each other (Holloman 1969: 173), with the result that some participants have a larger share than they gained by inheritance per se.

6. More generally, the existence or nonexistence of descent groups or descent categories in a given society is often neither obvious nor beyond dispute (Keesing 1970; Fox 1967a: 32–36), though we tend to assume the opposite.

7. For sources on this issue see the discussions and bibliographies in Hoben 1973; Fortes 1969; Keesing 1970; Goodenough 1970.

8. A few now also bury their members in family-owned plots. On my principal field site the communal graveyard serving the whole village has fallen into some disrepair in recent years, and some residents have taken to burying their kinsmen within jointly held coconut groves. The extent to which this trend can continue is limited by Cuna burial ritual, which requires that grave sites be located within a few yards of the principal river with which each village is associated.

9. It is perhaps significant that Cuna reckon kin connection in the same way regardless of whether they are discussing land-holding groups, and regardless of whether the particular informant belongs to one at all. Thus the statement that we "have the same grandfather" (*emar tan nikka*) can be used to explain why two cousins cannot marry each other, or why they share rights in a piece of land, or how they are related in general. This implies that, though the contrast between ancestor-focused and ego-focused *groups* is useful and valid, descent *reckoning* and kinship *reckoning* may not be as radically different as is sometimes asserted (cf. Scheffler 1973: 756–764).

References

Aberle, David, 1961. Matrilineal descent in cross-cultural perspective. In David Schneider and Kathleen Gough, eds., *Matrilineal Kinship*. Berkeley: University of California Press.

Fortes, Meyer, 1969. *Kinship and the Social Order*. Chicago: Aldine.

Fox, Robin, 1967a. *The Keresan Bridge: A Problem in Pueblo Ethnology*. New York: Humanities Press.

————, 1967b. *Kinship and Marriage: An Anthropological Perspective.* Harmondsworth, Middlesex: Penguin.

Goodenough, Ward, 1963. Review of *Matrilineal Kinship,* edited by David Schneider and Kathleen Gough. *American Anthropologist,* 65: 923–928.

————, 1970. *Description and Comparison in Cultural Anthropology.* Chicago: Aldine.

Gough, Kathleen, 1961. The modern disintegration of matrilineal descent groups. In David Schneider and Kathleen Gough, eds., *Matrilineal Kinship.* Berkeley: University of California Press.

Helms, Mary W., 1971. *Asang: Adaptations to Culture Contact in a Miskito Community.* Gainesville: University of Florida Press.

Hoben, Allen, 1973. *Land Tenure Among the Amhara of Ethiopia.* Chicago: University of Chicago Press.

Holloman, Regina, 1969. Developmental change in San Blas. Ph.D. dissertation, Northwestern University.

Howe, James, 1974. Village political organization among the San Blas Cuna. Ph.D. dissertation, University of Pennsylvania.

Keesing, Roger, 1970. Shrines, ancestors, and cognatic descent: the Kwaio and Tallensi. *American Anthropologist,* 72: 755–775.

Murdock, George P., 1949. *Social Structure.* New York: Free Press.

Naroll, Raoul, 1970. What have we learned from cross-cultural surveys? *American Anthropologist,* 72: 1227–1288.

Nordenskiöld, Erland, 1938. *An Historical and Ethnological Survey of the Cuna Indians,* S. Henry Wassén, ed. Comparative Ethnographical Studies, No. 10. Göteborg, Sweden: Etnografiska Museet.

Scheffler, Harold, 1973. Kinship, descent, and alliance. In John Honigmann, ed., *Handbook of Social and Cultural Anthropology.* Chicago: Rand McNally.

Service, Elman, 1971. *Primitive Social Organization: An Evolutionary Perspective.* 2d ed. New York: Random House.

Smith, M. G., 1962. *Kinship and Community in Carriacou.* New Haven: Yale University Press.

Solien, Nancie L., 1959. The nonunilineal descent group in the Caribbean and Central America. *American Anthropologist,* 61: 578–583.

Stephens, William, 1963. *The Family in Cross-Cultural Perspective.* New York: Holt, Rinehart and Winston.

Stout, David, 1947. *San Blas Cuna Acculturation: An Introduction.* Viking Fund Publications in Anthropology, No. 9. New York: Wenner-Gren Foundation for Anthropological Research.

Afterword: Anthropological Research
in Lower Central America

FRANKLIN O. LOVELAND

This Afterword attempts to summarize the results of a decade of recent research on lower Central America by a new generation of scholars and to suggest new directions for the decade ahead. Some of the results of this recent research are presented in the chapters in this volume, which clearly demonstrate that we have made progress toward understanding some of the ethnological problems that lower Central American societies present.

Over a decade ago, in 1964, Doris Stone presented a paper (1966) to the Thirty-Sixth International Congress of Americanists in which she outlined the state of Central American ethnology at that time, using Adams' (1957) categories of acculturation to list the impressive results of research done in the 1950s and early 1960s. Stone (1966: 17) concluded her comments with the following observation: "In this short summary referring to the present state of ethnology in Central America, the slow acculturation of the native towns is evident, as is, at the same time, the need for more detailed research before the highways and the power of the local authorities accelerate the process." Much has happened in the time since Stone presented her paper. A broad research base has been established, and there has been definite progress toward obtaining more detailed investigations of lower Central American societies. Some of the studies include: González (1969), Holloman (1969), Orso (1970), Kramer (1970), Sherzer (1970), Helms (1971), Young (1971), Costello (1972), Stone (1972), Nietschmann (1973), Wilson (1973), Howe (1974), and Loveland (1975).

However, much remains to be done. Nietschmann (1969: 98–99), among others, has observed that there are "many Indian groups in

Eastern Central America where initial as well as additional research is needed." In some areas we do not even have accurate census data or an adequate knowledge of the language spoken or the culture(s) of the inhabitants. For example, the different subgroups of Sumu and an isolated section of the Rama in the Punta Gorda River area of Nicaragua have never been studied. We know very little about the Guatuso and the peoples of northeastern Costa Rica. It is imperative that we strive to gain a basic knowledge of these peoples before their languages and lifestyles are transformed as a result of accelerated contact and rapid social change. Fortunately, Maria Eugenia Bozzoli de Wille (1969) and her students are attempting to provide basic information on the Indians in Costa Rica, but to my knowledge no one has attempted to do the same in such detail for the various subgroups of the Miskito and Sumu Indians in Nicaragua.

The chapters in this volume do bring new information to light. Initially one is struck by the comparative implications of much of this research. The essays by Helms, Howe, and Minelli, as well as my own chapter, fall into this category. Helms's chapter on the competition for succession to chiefly office in indigenous Panamanian chiefdoms contributes to our knowledge of political systems in rank societies and makes comparisons with some of the work done in Polynesian societies. This approach represents the kind of "external" comparison that is needed to fit lower Central American research into more general frames of reference. Helms's essay also reminds us that historical sources can be utilized by anthropologists to make meaningful ethnographic comparisons. Howe's chapter attacks another problem, that of descent groups. In examining his data on the Cuna, Howe pays careful attention to the implications of his research for the more detailed literature in social anthropology on the nature and origins of descent groups.

With regard to what we may call "internal" comparisons, that is, comparisons among lower Central American societies, my own chapter and the one by Minelli are illustrative. My exegesis of the myths and ceremony or ritual regarding the hunting, butchering, and eating of manatees among the Rama presents some internal comparisons between Miskito and Rama myths and ceremonies. Minelli examines the relationship between the Mexican-Mesoamerican heartland and the Talamancan-Guaymí hinterland with respect to specific cultural traits, and suggests the possibility that certain Mexican traits survived in this portion of the Intermediate Area. Her analysis is pertinent to the question of whether we must consider lower Central America as a frontier of Mesoamerica in some respects or whether these postulated relationships between the Talamancan-Guaymí area and the Mexican-Mesoamerican heartland are evidence of a more recent awareness of Latin American history among indigenous peoples.

Another problem facing researchers of lower Central American societies is the need for more detailed studies of social structure and social organization. The chapters by Cosminsky, Helms, Holloman, and Howe make valuable contributions in this area. For example, Cosminsky's essay on relationships among ethnic groups in Punta Gorda, Belize, details some of the factors which define ethnicity in this urban setting and attempts to explain the nature of interethnic social relationships. Holloman's chapter represents a first-rate contribution to the literature on the developmental cycle of domestic groups. These studies also indicate, however, that we have just begun to collate the data on social organization and social structure for lower Central American societies. For many of these groups (Sumu, Guatuso, Rama, Coastal Miskito, Boruca) there are no detailed studies of social organization and social structure. There is some evidence that the situation is changing, for a number of studies have recently begun.

Still another area of growing interest among researchers is the cosmology of lower Central American societies. The chapters by Young and myself deal specifically with aspects of cosmology, particularly with the problem of solidarity and conflict as it relates to myth and ceremony. Young's essay on *krun* illustrates the need to collect information on ceremonies which are falling into disuse. It is heartening to note that a symposium was held at the 1975 annual meeting of the American Anthropological Association on the topic of "Ritual and Symbolism in Indigenous Central America."

A further area of inquiry in lower Central American studies is that of cultural ecology and economics. In recent years a series of studies have been done on the Miskito by Nietschmann (1973) and Brian Weiss (1975). Michael Chibnik (personal communication) is presently engaged in an analysis of the economic strategies of part-time farmers in three villages in Belize, while Richard Costello (1972) has discussed some of the results of his research on the dual economy of the San Blas Cuna. Finally, there is Craig's (1966) monograph on the geography of fishing in Belize. All of these contributions to the growing literature in cultural ecology and economic anthropology represent a tangible advancement. Furthermore, these studies make it clear that ecological situations may vary significantly within a single cultural sphere. However, very little work has been done on other Central American cultures from the cultural ecological perspective. In this volume, Dorothy Cattle explores the nutritional status of the Miskito residents at Little Sandy Bay, while William Davidson's chapter represents a step toward understanding the nature of Black Carib habitats. However, the Talamanca, Cuna, Boruca, Guatuso, and Sumu have thus far remained relatively unexplored in cultural ecological terms. One would like to see more work done on coastal and riverine groups similar to the Miskito and the peoples of Belize. The east coast of Central America provides the cultural ecologist with a unique set of circumstances in which both the riverine-forest and ocean environments play important roles in shaping cultures.

As we consider the question "where do we go from here?" several additional points should be made. Naturally we need more extensive field work in lower Central America in the problem areas outlined above. However, another fundamental deficiency to date lies in our inadequate knowledge of the indigenous languages of the region. Too frequently we rely on Lehmann (1920) and others when in fact more sophisticated studies of these languages are needed in light of recent advances in linguistic theory. Hopefully researchers like Barbara Assadi, who has worked among the Rama, will be able to start us in the right direction by analyzing those indigenous languages on the verge of extinction and reanalyzing those languages for which old grammars are outdated. Work comparable to that of Sherzer (1970) and Howe (1972) for the Cuna should be replicated among other groups so that we have a broader linguistic base on which to build our ethnographic analyses.

In addition to field work, improved coordination of research efforts should be sought. Many lower Central American researchers pursue their interests individually and independently. We have not attempted to organize our research efforts or to pursue problems systematically. Greater communication is imperative so that investigators will be able to collaborate and to integrate their research strategies.

A few words also should be said concerning methodology. What kinds of questions should we be asking and how should we go about our analyses? We have extant data which could be used successfully in comparative analyses and historical reconstruction, but this possibility has not been explored. For example, we have a fairly good record of the kinship terminologies for lower Central American societies, and yet to date no one has attempted a comparative analysis either of the terms or of the wider social systems which they represent. Heath

(1927: 83–85) gives a detailed list of Miskito death names, but it remains unanalyzed. Cosmographies for all lower Central American societies should be mapped and rituals should be observed and noted down in detail as Young has done for the Guaymí. Do we not have a chance to add considerably to our general knowledge of the processes and structures of New World mythologies in this middle zone between South America and the north?

In short, lower Central American anthropology must recognize and deal with a wide range of questions and issues. The prospect is exciting. In a still largely unknown area, no one knows what future research may find.

References

Adams, Richard N., 1957. *Cultural Surveys of Panama—Nicaragua—Guatemala—El Salvador—Honduras*. Washington, D.C.: Pan American Sanitary Bureau, World Health Organization.

Bozzoli de Wille, Maria Eugenia, 1969. *Localidades indigenas costaricenses 1960–68*. Publicaciones de la Universidad de Costa Rica, Serie Misc., No. 133. San José: Ciudad Universitaria, Rodrigo Facio.

Costello, Richard W., 1972. The dual economy in a San Blas community: Rio Azucar. Paper read at the 71st Annual Meeting of the American Anthropological Association, Toronto.

Craig, Alan K., 1966. *Geography of Fishing in British Honduras and Adjacent Coastal Waters*. Coastal Studies Series, No. 14. Baton Rouge: Louisiana State University.

González, Nancie L. Solien, 1969. *Black Carib Household Structure: A Study of Migration and Modernization*. American Ethnological Society Monograph No. 48. Seattle: University of Washington Press.

Heath, George R., 1927. *Grammar of the Miskito Language*. Herrnhut, East Germany: F. Lindenbein.

Helms, Mary W., 1971. *Asang: Adaptations to Culture Contact in a Miskito Community*. Gainesville: University of Florida Press.

Holloman, Regina, 1969. Developmental change in San Blas. Ph.D. dissertation, Northwestern University.

Howe, James, 1972. Carrying the village: Cuna political metaphors. Unpublished manuscript.

————, 1974. Village political organization among the San Blas Cuna. Ph.D. dissertation, University of Pennsylvania.

Kramer, Fritz, 1970. *The Literature of the Cuna Indians*. Etnologiska Studier, No. 30. Göteborg, Sweden: Etnografiska Museet.

Lehmann, Walter, 1920. *Zentral Amerika*. Berlin: Dietrich Reimer.

Loveland, Franklin O., 1975. Order and disorder in Rama cosmology: dialectical aspects of natural symbols among the Rama Indians of eastern Nicaragua. Ph.D. dissertation, Duke University.

Nietschmann, Bernard, 1969. The distribution of Miskito, Sumu, and Rama

Indians, eastern Nicaragua. *Bulletin of the International Committee on Urgent Anthropological and Ethnological Research,* 11: 91–102.
———, 1973. *Between Land and Water.* New York: Seminar Press.
Nietschmann, Bernard, and Judi Nietschmann, 1972. I Rama—comunitá indígena del Nicaragua. *Terra Ameriga,* 23–24: 7–12.
Orso, Ethelyn, 1970. *Hot and Cold in the Folk Medicine of the Island of Chira, Costa Rica.* Latin American Studies Institute Monograph and Dissertation Series, No. 1. Baton Rouge: Louisiana State University.
Sherzer, Joel, 1970. Talking backwards in Cuna: the sociological reality of phonological descriptions. *Southwestern Journal of Anthropology,* 26: 343–353.
Stone, Doris, 1966. El estado actual de la etnologia en la America Central. *Actas del XXXVI Congreso Internacional de Americanistas.* Vol. 3. Barcelona.
———, 1972. *Pre-Columbian Man Finds Central America.* Cambridge, Mass.: Peabody Museum.
Weiss, Brian, 1975. *Selling a Subsistence System.* 16 mm. color film. Sherman Oaks, Calif.: B and C Films.
Wilson, Peter, 1973. *Crab Antics.* New Haven: Yale University Press.
Young, Philip, 1971. *Ngawbe: Tradition and Change Among the Western Guaymí of Panama.* Urbana: University of Illinois Press.

INDEX

Index